THE LIBRARY OF HOLOCAUST TESTIMONIES

Surviving the Nazis, Exile and Siberia

To Paul best wishes

Edith Sekules

Belfast 21.2.2001.

The Library of Holocaust Testimonies

Editors: Antony Polonsky, Martin Gilbert CBE, Aubrey Newman,
Raphael F. Scharf, Ben Helfgott

Under the auspices of the Yad Vashem Committee of the Board of
Deputies of British Jews and the Centre for Holocaust Studies,
University of Leicester

My Lost World by Sara Rosen
From Dachau to Dunkirk by Fred Pelican
Breathe Deeply, My Son by Henry Wermuth
My Private War by Jacob Gerstenfeld-Maltiel
A Cat Called Adolf by Trude Levi
An End to Childhood by Miriam Akavia
A Child Alone by Martha Blend
I Light a Candle by Gena Turgel
My Heart in a Suitcase by Anne L. Fox
Memoirs from Occupied Warsaw, 1942-1945
by Helena Szereszewska
Have You Seen My Little Sister?
by Janina Fischler-Martinho
Surviving the Nazis, Exile and Siberia by Edith Sekules
Out of the Ghetto by Jack Klajman with Ed Klajman
From Thessaloniki to Auschwitz and Back 1926-1996
by Erika Myriam Kounio Amariglio
Translated by Theresa Sundt
I Was No. 20832 at Auschwitz by Eva Tichauer
Translated by Colette Lévy and Nicki Rensten
My Child is Back! by Ursula Pawel
Wartime Experiences in Lithuania by Rivka Lozansky Bogomolnaya
Translated by Miriam Beckerman

Surviving the Nazis, Exile and Siberia

EDITH SEKULES

VALLENTINE MITCHELL
LONDON • PORTLAND, OR

First published in 2000 in Great Britain by
VALLENTINE MITCHELL
Crown House, 47 Chase Side, Southgate
London, N14 5BP

and in the United States of America by
VALLENTINE MITCHELL
c/o ISBS, 5804 N.E. Hassalo Street
Portland, Oregon 97213-3644

Website: http://www.vmbooks.com

Copyright © 2000 Erika Myriam Kounio Amariglio
Reprinted 2001

British Library Cataloguing in Publication Data
Sekules, Edith
  Surviving the Nazis, Exile and Siberia – (The library of Holocaust testimonies)
  1. Sekules, Edith
  2. Holocaust, Jewish (1939–1945) – Personal narratives 3. Jewish women – Austria
  – Vienna – Biography
  I. Title
  940.5'318'092

ISBN 0-85303-3900
ISSN 1363-3759

Library of Congress Cataloging-in-Publication Data

Sekules, Edith, 1916–
Surviving the Nazis, Exile and Siberia / Edith Sekules.
    p. cm. (The library of Holocaust testimonies, ISSN 1363-3759)
  ISBN 0-85303-388-9 (pbk.)
    1. Sekules, Edith, 1916– 2. Jews – Austria – Vienna – Biography. 3. Holocaust,
Jewish (1939–1945) – Austria – Vienna – Personal narratives. 4. Refugees,
Jewish–Soviet Union – Biography. 5. Holocaust survivors – Northern Ireland –
Biography. 6. Jews – Northern Ireland – Biography. 7. Vienna (Austria) –
Biography. 8. Soviet Union – Biography. 9. Northern Ireland – Biography.
I. Title.

DS135.A93 S43 2000
940.53'092–dc21
[B]   99-086422

All rights reserved. No part of this publication may be reproduced, stored in or introduced into a retrieval system or transmitted in any form or by any means, electronic, mechanical, photocopying, recording or otherwise, without the prior written permission of the publisher of this book.

Printed in Great Britain by Anthony Rowe Ltd, Eastbourne.

Contents

List of Illustrations — vii

Biographical Note — viii

Edith Sekules' Family Tree — x

Maps — xii

Prologue — 1

Part 1 – Farewell to Youth, Vienna: 1916–38
1. The First Goodbye: August 1938 — 5
2. My Forebears — 8
3. Early Childhood: 1916–24 — 11
4. Schooldays: 1924–31 — 16
5. A Change of Direction: 1931–32 — 25
6. The Hotel Bristol: 1932–38 — 30
7. The Second Goodbye: 1938 — 42
8. Reflections on Vienna — 48

Part 2 – Exile: 1938–47
9. Estonia: September 1938–June 1941 — 53
10. Harju Camp, Estonia: July 1941 — 70
11. Oranki Camp, Gorki: July–November 1941 — 75

12.	Aktyubinsk Camp, Kazakhstan: November 1941–July 1942	79
13.	Spaski Camp, Karaganda: July 1942–January 1943	89
14.	Kok U Sek Camp, Karaganda: January 1943–May 1945	92
15.	Post-war Detention, Kok U Sek Camp: May 1945–January 1947	108
16.	The Long Trek Home, Karaganda to Vienna: January–March 1947	116
17.	Vienna: March–September 1947	122

Part 3 – Never Say, 'I Can't'; Say, 'I'll Try': 1947–99

18.	London: September–October 1947	129
19.	Londonderry: October 1947–December 1949	132
20.	Kilkeel – The Early Years: 1950–55	138
21.	A Phase of Development: 1956–70	149
22.	A Phase of Growth: 1971–74	155
23.	A House of our Own	157
24.	Winding Down: 1976–91	159
25.	Postscript	162

List of Illustrations

Between pages 80 and 81

1. Edith with her mother and Lotte, 1918.
2. Mother, father, Kurt and Edith, Vienna, 1934.
3. The aircraft that brought Edith and family to Tallinn, 1938.
4. Edith with Ruth, two, and baby Walter, Estonia, 1940.
5. Official photograph of Edith with Leah, two, Walter, seven, Ruth, nine, and Kurt, Vienna 1947.
6. From left to right: Leah, Edith, Ruth, Kurt with Esther, and Walter, Kilkeel, 1954.
7. Brian Faulkener, Northern Ireland Minister of Commerce, visits the Company's stand in Gothenburg, Sweden, 1968.
8. Edith and Kurt celebrate their golden wedding, 1986.
9. Golden wedding present; a photograph of the family with staff at the foot of the Mourne Mountains, 1986.
10. Peak of achievement; a small selection of customer labels.
11. Edith introduces Walter to The Princess Royal at the Men's International Fashion Fair, Paris, 1989.
12. Enjoying their retirement; Edith and Kurt on holiday in the Bahamas, 1996.

Biographical Note

Edith Sekules was born in Vienna in 1916, where she spent a happy childhood and had interesting work until 1938. Hitler's invasion of Austria marked the starting point of nine years of exile, including six years spent in various Siberian camps.

After she returned to Europe in 1947, she set about rebuilding her life in Northern Ireland, raising four children and creating knitwear production with worldwide sales.

Since 1991 she has been enjoying retirement with her husband, travelling, gardening and relishing her fourteen grandchildren and great-grandchildren.

The Library of Holocaust Testimonies

It is greatly to the credit of Frank Cass that this series of survivors' testimonies is being published in Britain. The need for such a series has long been apparent here, where many survivors made their homes.

Since the end of the war in 1945 the terrible events of the Nazi destruction of European Jewry have cast a pall over our time. Six million Jews were murdered within a short period; the few survivors have had to carry in their memories whatever remains of the knowledge of Jewish life in more than a dozen countries, in several thousand towns, in tens of thousands of villages, and in innumerable families. The precious gift of recollection has been the sole memorial for millions of people whose lives were suddenly and brutally cut off.

For many years, individual survivors have published their testimonies. But many more have been reluctant to do so, often because they could not believe that they would find a publisher for their efforts.

In my own work over the past two decades, I have been approached by many survivors who had set down their memories in writing, but who did not know how to have them published. I realized what a considerable emotional strain the writing down of such hellish memories had been. I also realized, as I read many dozens of such accounts, how important each account was, in its own way, in recounting aspects of the story that had not been told before, and adding to our understanding of the wide range of human suffering, struggle and aspiration.

With so many people and so many places involved, including many hundreds of camps, it was inevitable that the historians and students of the Holocaust should find it difficult at times to grasp the scale and range of events. The publication of memoirs is therefore an indispensable part of the extension of knowledge, and of public awareness of the crimes that had been committed against a whole people.

Martin Gilbert
Merton College, Oxford

Edith Sekules' Family Tree

MY FATHER'S FAMILY

Ludwig Mendel —— m. —— Anna Schmelkes
(1854–1935)   1879   (1854–1940)

Eugen (my father)   Frieda
(1881–1940)   (1883–1952)

MY MOTHER'S FAMILY

Joseph Bielitz — m. — Mathilde Bell — — m.(2)   Laura
(1860–1921)   1889   (1865–1905)   1906 (1870–1943)

Fritz   Marianne   Lise   Hansi (Joan)
         (my mother)
(1891–1943) (1894–1969) (1896–1930)   (1907–1984)

x

MY PARENTS AND FAMILY

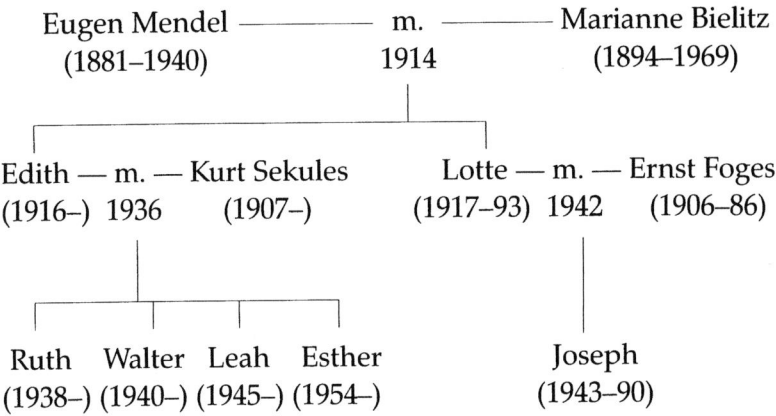

MY HUSBAND'S FAMILY

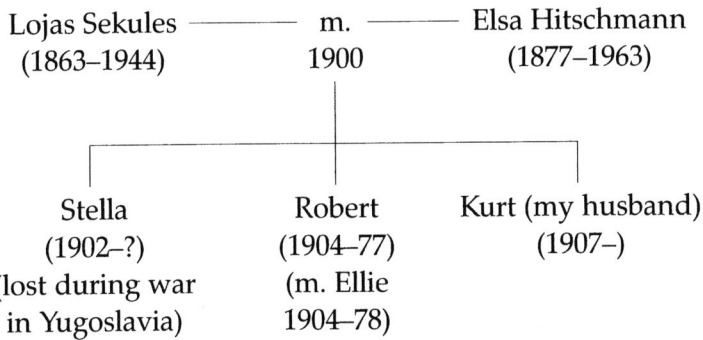

Maps

HARJU CAMP TO ORANKI CAMP
(750 miles approx.)

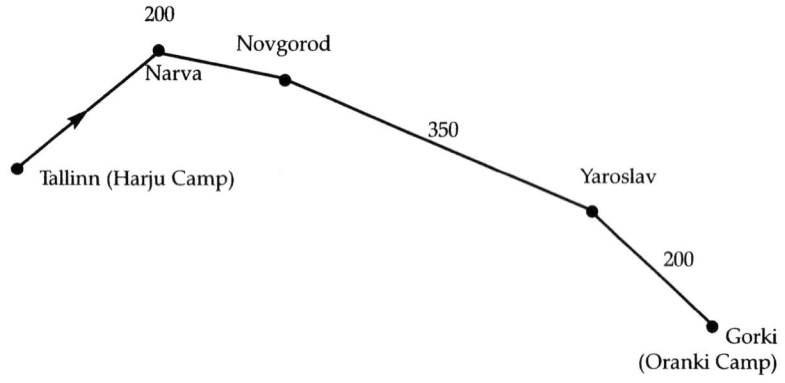

miles

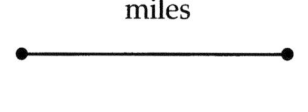

ORANKI CAMP TO AKTYUBINSK CAMP
(800 miles approx.)

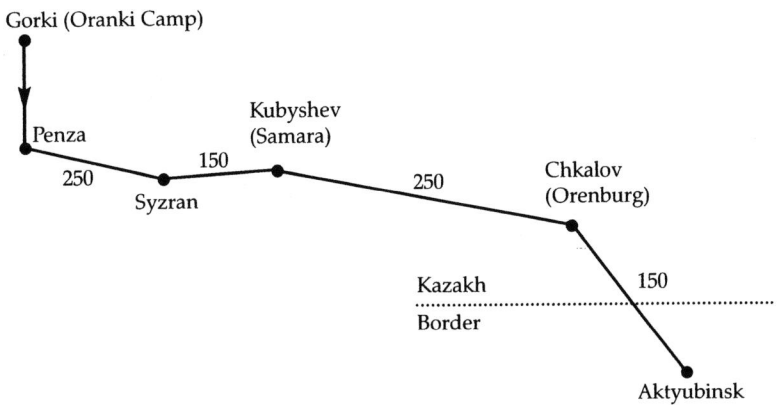

AKTYUBINSK CAMP TO SPASKI CAMP
(1,000 miles approx.)

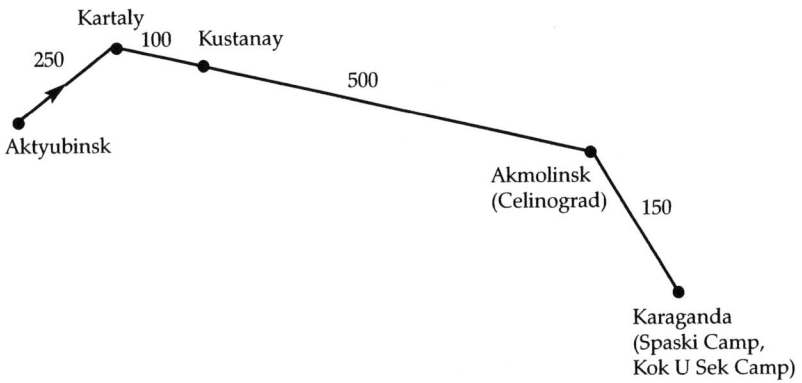

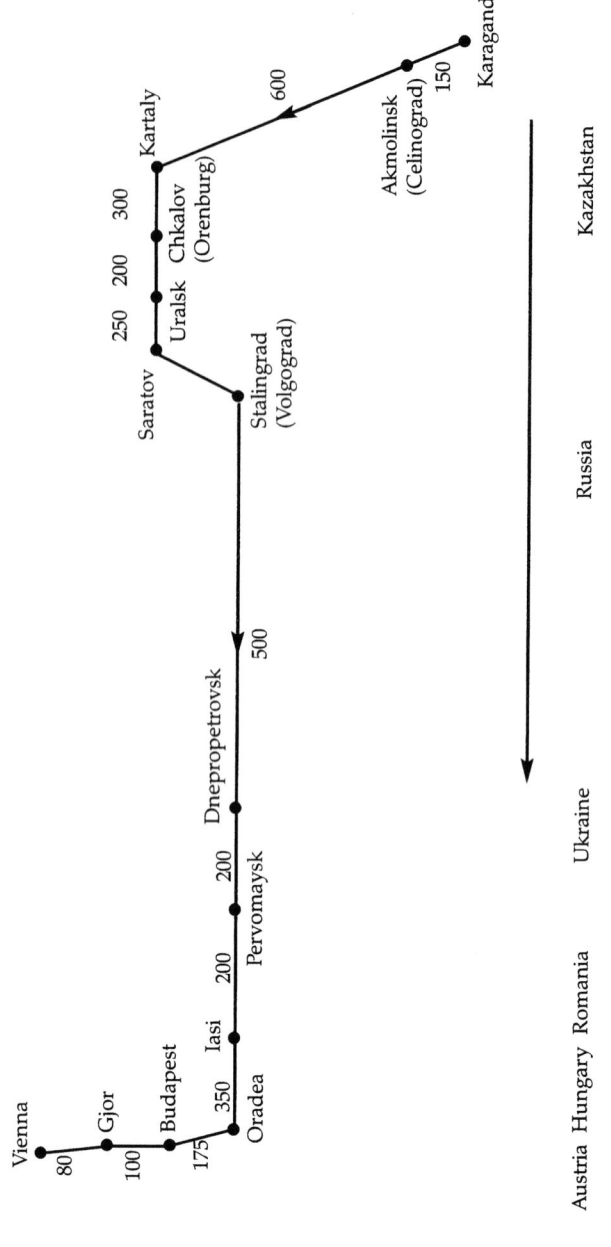

THE JOURNEY HOME (3,350 miles approx.)

Acknowledgements

There is one person to whom I wish to express my deepest gratitude. It is my friend Peter O'Hara, who did not give up until he found the right publisher.

Peter's encouragement, enthusiasm and active help with research have made it possible to write my story down and give it shape. In addition to his personal involvement, he had the help of his charming wife Maura. Other members of his family helped in the production of discs and the enhancement of photographs. They all helped to make my cherished dream come true.

Prologue

8 June 1999

Today, as I celebrate my 83rd birthday, the panoramic view of the Mourne Mountains from our home in Kilkeel, County Down, is more stunning than usual. The strong summer sunshine, with a crystal-clear blue sky, provides an impressive backdrop to the dark and severe shapes of the mountain peaks. The sight of cattle and sheep grazing in the lowland fields enhances the peace and serenity of this beautiful part of Northern Ireland. It is a very fitting place to live out the later chapters in the story of the difficult and eventful journey of my life.

My journey began on 8 June 1916 when I was born into a family which was part of the vibrant Jewish culture of Vienna. That world was shattered for ever by the Nazis in 1938 and it is difficult now to visualise how utterly different everything was in those far-off days. The saddest difference for me is, of course, the absence of the thousands of Jewish people who contributed to every aspect of European society. In my youth there were almost 200,000 Jews in Vienna; now there are only a few thousand.

In a century which has included a series of holocausts from the First World War through the Stalinist purges, the Second World War, the Chinese famines and Cambodia through to

Rwanda and Yugoslavia, I became a victim and survivor of the worst ethnic cleansing of all – the Shoah, the Jewish Holocaust of the Second World War.

I feel exceptionally lucky to have survived, through fortuitous circumstances, whilst millions of Jews perished. I have decided to tell my story because I believe that everything relevant, however small, which adds to the texture of memory of that horrific period adds to our stature as a people. When I recall my schooldays and young adulthood in Vienna, it is deeply saddening to focus on how our diverse and sophisticated culture was obliterated in a few short years and on how many of my classmates, friends and colleagues disappeared – presumably to their deaths in the extermination camps. My story is dedicated to their memory.

In the immediate post-war years I felt extremely bitter and disliked all things German. I felt then that Austria was much too beautiful a country for Austrians, and could never accept that Jews should resettle there or in Germany. However, as I got older my resentments faded although, over the years, articles, books and programmes about the Holocaust and about the widespread complicity of so many people and organisations rekindled them.

Nevertheless, I retain great affection for my beloved Vienna and for Salzburg, which I visit as frequently as I can. Both cities have a very different feel from that of the 1930s, when Jewish culture and presence was pronounced, particularly in the arts and in commerce.

Time, of course, is a great healer and mellower, but I believe we must be vigilant and, as Steven Spielberg is helping to ensure, we must never forget. Forgiving is another matter.

Part 1

Farewell to Youth
Vienna: 1916–38

1 · *The First Goodbye: August 1938*

It was August 1938. I stood with my parents and younger sister Lottchen on the crowded platform of Vienna's Westbahnhof awaiting the departure announcement. Soon Lottchen would board the train which would take her on the long journey to England and an uncertain and unknown future. When it came time for her to board the carriage we all kissed her goodbye and wished her *'bon voyage'*. The tears welled up because all of us suspected that we might never see her again. I still see clearly her sad and apprehensive face as she looked back from the top of the carriage steps. It created one of the lasting memories of my life. As the train crept slowly out of the station we all waved our handkerchiefs and Lottchen waved back. That was the moment when our close-knit family was broken up for ever.

Lottchen – or Lotte as we called her – was the first of our family to escape the hell which Vienna had become for its Jewish people. In the few months after the Nazi annexation in March 1938, Jews had been stripped of all dignity and had been taken aback at the strength of hatred and collusion of the local non-Jewish population. Anyone whom the Nazis considered Jewish-looking was totally demeaned and forced to carry out degrading acts such as the scrubbing of graffiti off the pavements on their hands and knees; others were arbitrarily chosen for imprisonment in the concentration camps. Many Jewish businesses were smeared with slogans such as 'Do not buy from the Jew!' whilst many non-Jewish shops displayed a sign saying 'Jews not admitted!' Very rapidly the whole of Jewish business and society disintegrated.

Lotte was twenty-one that year and full of youthful confidence. She believed that all would be well in the end and that her life in England would be a temporary phase. She had spent two summers in Margate acting as an au pair for a family with four children and thus knew something of England. After the Nazi invasion she was full of hope that this English family would help and so she wrote to them in late spring. Sadly, they declined to get involved. This merely toughened Lotte's resolve and she set about obtaining a permit for nursing training in London. Her other occcupation option in the UK was domestic work, provided a specific job was lined up, usually by the Jewish Refugee Agency.

She showed courage and determination by frequently queuing for hours at the British Embassy, at the Refugee Agency and at Gestapo Headquarters in the Hotel Metropole until she acquired the necessary documents. She had to obtain a passport, a visa and a work permit, as well as certificates of clearance on taxes, and to state that she had no criminal record. The whole process proved tortuous for her because all the offices were under great pressure due to the large numbers of Jews and 'politicals' seeking to get out of the Reich.

Lotte was good-natured throughout. She enjoyed the farewell family gathering in our home in the Alserstrasse on the evening before her departure for England, when she was the centre of attention. We all consoled her and flitted around reminding her to check that she had packed everything. All she had were a few clothes, books, photographs, her cherished Box Tengor camera and ten D-Marks. This was the maximum amount of money which an emigrant was allowed to take out of the country.

The First Goodbye: August 1938

As she was leaving the Alserstrasse for the last time, Lotte stole a last tearful glance at our apartment block which had been home for her for 15 years. She brightened up on the tram journey to the Westbahnhof when we all reminisced about those times when this train station was the starting point of our joyous holidays in the Tirol and in the Salzkammergut. The station was crowded and had lines of emigrants queuing for clearance. After Lotte's luggage was searched thoroughly by the Gestapo, she had to endure a body search to check if she was hiding forbidden exports, such as jewellery or money. Her only bright moment came when the watch that father had given her as a farewell present was not confiscated.

On the tram journey back home very little was said as each of us dwelt on the sadness of the occasion. When we reached home, I went to Lotte's abandoned room, sat down on her bed and cried. I thought of how she had lit up my life over the years with her cheerfulness and courage and of how I might never see her again. Our sheltered youth had come to an abrupt and merciless end!

2 · My Forebears

Lotte and I were both children of the Great War. I was born in Vienna in 1916 and Lotte a year later. Our parents had married six months before the outbreak of war in 1914.

Both parents came from affluent *Bodenständig* Jewish families – those who had come to Vienna in the last century and now formed part of the indigenous population. They had assimilated into the city's emancipated and pluralist society and, in the years prior to the First World War, were making great contributions to all areas of a vibrant and cultured city at the heart of a great empire. That situation was to change for ever.

Our families were regarded as part of the 'middle set' and lived in the better Jewish quarters, such as the Textile Quarter, which bordered the Danube Canal on the north and north-east of the city. They tended not to mix with the Jewish 'upper set' out in Hitzing in the south-west, the very rich in their Ringstrasse apartments, or with the poor Eastern Jews, the *Ostjuden*, who had fled from persecution and had settled in the Leopoldstadt district, east of the canal. The *Ostjuden* had remained fundamentalist and orthodox and had not assimilated into the wider culture.

My maternal grandfather, Joseph Bielitz, came as a young man to Vienna from Papa in western Hungary in the 1880s.

My Forebears

He was almost the same age as his cousin Theodor Herzl who had also been born in Hungary, lived in Austria and became the founder of the Zionist movement. Joseph got his first job in my great-grandmother Bell's business, which wholesaled boys' ready-made clothing. He fell in love with her daughter, Mathilde, and they married in 1889. Eventually grandfather started his own business importing cloth from Czechoslovakia. Joseph and Mathilde worked extremely hard, lived modestly, and became successful. They had three children, Fritz, Marianne (my mother) and Lise. Sadly, my grandmother died in 1905. Grandfather remarried and another daughter was born. He lived until 1921; by then all his savings had become worthless war bonds.

My paternal grandparents both came to Vienna from Czechoslovakia in the 1870s – my grandmother, Anna Schmelkes, from Prague and my grandfather, Ludwig Mendel, from Kolin, just east of Prague. Their ability to speak German fluently enabled them to succeed quickly and, although from strictly religious Jewish homes in Czechoslovakia, they integrated fully into Viennese society. Both were twenty-five when they married in 1879, when grandfather was running a horse-drawn transport business in partnership with his brother. The partnership tensions caused grandfather to retire early from the business. My grandparents then bought a large townhouse on Lustandlgasse, near the Volksopera. They occupied one of the ten apartments in the property and lived from the rent of the rest. They had two children, Eugen (my father) and Frieda. Grandfather died in 1935 aged eighty-one and grandmother in 1940, aged eighty-six.

My father, Eugen Mendel, was born in 1881 in Vienna. He was a very talented young man, good at piano, drawing, sports and languages. However, it must have been his parents who advised him to study engineering, regarding it as a safer basis for his future than all the artistic aspirations. After graduating in 1902 he obtained his first job at a motor car factory in Gjoer in Hungary. Among other duties he was test-driving the new models. I still cherish his photo in his motoring outfit – a long coat, headgear and goggles. After a few years he came back to Vienna and entered a firm of motor factors.

Eugen met my mother, Marianne Bielitz, for the first time in 1913 when she was nineteen and he was thirty-two. They were both extremely attractive young people and it was not surprising that they quickly fell in love. My mother was then training to be a dressmaker and was expert at white embroidery. However, she was so keen to marry Eugen that she did not finish her apprenticeship, and within a year they were married.

My parents spent their honeymoon on the Adriatic at Abbazia, which was the smart place to go in those days. They returned to an apartment on the Schopenhauerstrasse in the north-west of the city. It was now full of the beautiful items brought to the marriage by my mother. It was a dowry of bedding, clothing, furniture and tableware worthy of a princess. The furniture, all custom-built, included a bedroom in Louis XVI style, oak in the dining room with a 12-seater table and a drawing room in contemporary secessionist style in mahogany. Her trousseau included dozens of hand-embroidered monogrammed pure linen sets of ladies' underwear, which were very fashionable in 1914. The table linen, bed linen and the bath and hand towels were in neat stacks each tied with yellow silk ribbons. The Rosenthal 12-place dinner set and the silver cutlery and cut glasses were regarded as so precious that they were produced only on special occasions.

It was into this comfortable and cultured world that I was born two years later.

3 · Early Childhood: 1916–24

My earliest memories are of the hustle and bustle in our street which comprised small apartment houses but no shops. Each house had a caretaker who lived with his family on the ground floor. They observed all comings and goings and were the eyes and ears of the community. At 10 o'clock at night the door was locked. If anyone returned late without a key the caretaker or his wife opened up for a fee.

All over the city at that time there were messenger stations, manned by ex-servicemen who couldn't find other work. These messengers, or *Dienstmänner*, wore red caps with an identification number and could be hired to deliver letters, small packages or flowers. They were a regular sight in every street. However, the saddest memory of my childhood was the distressing sight of war invalids begging and selling matches and shoelaces to eke out an existence. The state had treated its war heroes very shabbily.

Mother told me that, at birth, I was as red and thin as a skinned hare and was the first newborn baby she had ever seen. I quickly filled out and developed into an aware, but podgy, toddler whom she tended to spoil. Lotte, however, became a slow and dreamy child, a characteristic which mother found irritating. She often smacked Lotte for being so tardy and would then laugh when the child was howling, more from wounded pride than from pain. Mealtimes were the most constant battle area when mother would force Lotte to stay in her seat until she had finished her meal, which by then would be cold. It was most unpleasant to have to eat dishes such as cold spinach. At that time, mother did not realise that Lotte was a slow eater because she was troubled with adenoids and associated breathing difficulties. These confrontations drove Lotte closer to our first nanny, 'Mingi', to whom she became very attached and dependent on. Nanny was very fond of her, liked to spoil her and often told her fairy-tales late into the night.

Father had a handsome friendly face and a very outgoing and fun-loving nature, particularly when he was with mother and the two of us. Even from a young age we knew and felt that our parents were very happy and content, as was evident from their frequent use of pet names for each other. Father, of course, introduced us to all his musical interests. He played the piano frequently and concentrated on operas, particularly Wagner. It was this early involvement which created my lifelong love of music, opera and ballet. We also thought him a great storyteller and I can still conjure up my eager anticipation as we awaited patiently at night for his return from the movies. He would sit on the edge of our beds and relate colourfully the whole story, and more, of the film he had seen. He loved Chaplin, Harold Lloyd, Pat and Patachon but, most of all, those musical spectaculars with the large casts of pretty girls.

We lived in the Schopenhauerstrasse until 1923, when I was seven. The three-roomed apartment was spacious for a young couple but rather small when two growing children were added. We then moved up in the world to a larger home nearer the city centre. Apart from my thoughts of father and mother, my abiding memories of life during those seven years centre on my early schooldays, on summer holidays and on visits to our relatives.

Early Childhood: 1916–24

My first school was the General School in Martinstrasse which was just five minutes' walk from home. This was a local authority school and I remember clearly that the classroom was lit by gas lamps and the walls decorated with Junior Red Cross posters, reminding us to wash our hands and brush our teeth and giving various other pieces of good advice.

After music, reading was my great love. Lotte and I were the children who missed the greatest number of days from school because we were kept at home for the slightest cough, cold or sore throat. Then one of a dozen herbal teas was administered along with hot or cold compresses. I was delighted at these opportunities to read all day. We had a subscription for the Junior Red Cross magazine, which was a high-class publication full of good illustrations and stories. I devoured every issue and remember especially those in later years in memory of the centenaries in 1927 and 1928 of Beethoven's and Schubert's deaths. In 1928 Vienna went crazy with memorabilia in memory of Schubert – most of it kitschy and in bad taste, such as busts of him made from soap.

When I was four I was given a special treat by my grandparents Bielitz. They took me on a holiday to the beautiful spa, Baden bei Wien, about an hour by tram from the capital. My first impression was a strong smell of rotten eggs. The fact was that Baden was a favourite spa since Roman times because of its hot sulphur springs. I was taken twice to the open-air arena in the park. First I saw *The Merry Widow*; I can still visualise some of the scenery. The second opera was *The Gypsy Baron*. All I remember is a rider galloping on to the stage sitting back to front on a horse. A year later grandfather died of a heart attack. I was desolate because I loved him so much.

In the summer of 1922 I learnt to swim. The following holidays, in 1923, our parents took us to the Adriatic Sea at Porto Rose. We had a wonderful time, making sandcastles, collecting shells and, with my new-found confidence, swimming far out into the sea, to mother's despair. However it proved to be a tragic summer for us. My father developed pneumonia and had to be taken to hospital. Although he recovered it was established that he also suffered from tuberculosis and was sent immediately to a sanatorium in Switzerland.

After father left for Switzerland in 1923, and was to stay away for a whole year, it was decided that we needed a larger apartment so that, on his return, he could have a room of his own. We moved to a modern five-roomed apartment in the Alserstrasse, in the Alsergrund district.

Father's illness changed our lives forever. During his year away in sanatoria, mother had to cope alone including having to organise the move, in late 1923, to a larger apartment. Our building was in the main street of the district, with many big shops and two cinemas. As this was a main tram route, it was easy to reach all parts of the city. However, after moving from a suburban street with less traffic, it took some time to get used to the clanking of the tramcars late into the night and to the brightness of the street lamps which shone into our bedroom.

The new apartment was, of course, much more expensive than our previous one. Father's illness was costing a lot of money and, because he was forced to take things very easy, he could not maintain his previous earnings' level. From then on we were in continual financial difficulties. However, I always credited mother for resisting any lowering of her standards, particularly in respect of our education, where she refused to economise.

Lotte and I were transferred to another wonderful local authority General School on Pelikangasse, which was very near our apartment block. The school had about a hundred pupils and, as we moved to the next higher class, our teachers moved with us. Lotte and I were very fond of them. At home we had a French teacher who came twice each week.

Early Childhood: 1916–24

Mother delighted in decorating the new apartment. She had very good style and taste, which everyone admired, and loved modern decor, fabrics and furniture. I can recall vividly the cheerful pattern of waterfalls and little birds which she chose for our nursery – I have found that the childhood mind always registers clearly the decor of the nursery. We also had our own built-in wash-hand basin, which was very advanced for that time.

After some months in the sanatorium in Arosa, father was moved to one in a resort in the Austrian Tirol, which was less expensive than Switzerland and easier to reach from Vienna. When he stayed at Arosa, mother could visit him only once, whereas we could now visit him more easily. It was during this time that a very good family friend, Bernhard Altmann, provided the transport for our journeys to the Tirol. Bernhard was to play a vital role in my later life.

Shortly after my eighth birthday in the summer of 1924, father came home from the Tirol. What had been a difficult and traumatic year for our parents seemed exciting and new to Lotte and me.

4 · Schooldays: 1924–31

Father's return in late 1924 brought everything back to normal again. After a year in sanatoria he was used to having his own room and thus took to the larger apartment, which mother had furnished so well. He soon went back to his business and mother continued to help him by working in his office. Shortly after he returned, tensions with his associate began to arise and eventually the associate was replaced by mother's brother-in-law, Erwin Basch.

The summer holidays of 1925, when I was nine, were especially enjoyable. Father's strength had returned and he was able to take part in most of the activities. We had gone to a small village near Innsbruck where the scenery was glorious and the weather constantly sunny. One day, out of the blue, the whole family received an invitation from our good friend Bernhard Altmann to join him and his family on a trip which would take us by car through Switzerland and then over the Alps to the Italian lakes. Bernhard was so successful by then that he had two cars – a Chrysler and a Daimler – and was the only person in our social circle to have a car.

During those years education was of paramount importance to our parents and, apart from our school subjects, they insisted we should have as broad and cultured an education as possible. It thus became much more costly. Lessons in dancing,

Schooldays: 1924–31

French and piano had to be paid for. In 1926, at ten, I entered the Music Conservatoria and felt really grown up as I went alone on the tram journey of about half an hour. I really enjoyed every aspect of it and developed a girlish 'crush' on my piano teacher. I hoped to follow her example and become a concert pianist and rushed through my school homework every day to devote as much time as possible to piano practice.

My love of music, opera and theatre was enhanced by the involvement of various members of the family. Lotte and I loved to invent short plays and perform them for father and mother. Often we argued over our roles and I usually won any fights we had, being much the stronger. She would call me very hurtful names and often kept shouting 'I'll kill you.' If father heard this he would storm in and chastise her. Aunt Frieda, father's sister, also prepared plays with us for various family celebrations and her husband wrote witty parodies. In one performance of a play we almost set the place on fire when we put red crepe paper over the light bulb to indicate hell in a scene when Dr Faust meets Mephisto.

Music and opera became my main interests, ahead of reading and the theatre. My interest in playing the piano never faltered and Aunt Frieda often made me play with her a large repertory of classical music set for four hands. It was much later before I acknowledged the enormous value that this forced exercise was to my musical appreciation. Another great mile-stone on my musical journey was my first visit to the Staatsoper – the Vienna State Opera – to see *Hansel and Gretel* and *Die Puppenfee* ('The Fairy of the Dolls'). Everything about that event, on a Saturday before Christmas 1926, when I was ten, felt fantastic at the time and looking back over more than 70 years it still feels the same. It was the moment I became hooked on opera.

The year 1927 was a deeply traumatic one for Vienna, and I remember the tension that pervaded everything. It began in

January when three members of the anti-socialist front *Kämpfers* murdered two communists. All through the spring and early summer the city was full of small meetings and there were posters everywhere.

Everything became more difficult through the summer of that year. In June, shortly after my eleventh birthday, I contracted diphtheria. In July came the riots which were triggered by the acquittal of the three anti-socialists tried for the January murder of the two communists. The communist press called for the killing of judges and other public servants. Thousands took to the streets, looting and setting fire to many buildings. The Palace of Justice was stormed and set alight by a crowd estimated at over 10,000. Throughout the city the police fired machine guns at rioters who retaliated with rifle fire. Father, whose business premises on Bartensteingasse were quite near the major riot at the Palace of Justice, narrowly escaped a fusillade. Each day, as soon as we heard the paper boys on the Alserstrasse shout 'special edition', someone went and purchased a copy to learn about the latest trouble in the streets. As conditions were worsening, Chancellor Seipel called out the army, the Volkswehr, to back up the police. A general strike was declared and, with many of the Viennese in the army mutinying, the Chancellor called in troops from the provinces who helped quell the riots by the middle of July. In the end 80 people died and the whole episode started a German demand to annex Austria.

Over those few weeks my condition worsened. I could not breathe properly. As there was neither immunisation nor any drugs to cure diphtheria 70 years ago, a children's surgeon was called in to perform an emergency operation. He was a famous professor who was regarded as the most senior in his speciality. I remember him mainly for his beard. He asked mother to assist him. As I sat on a chair, he put a mask over my nose and mouth and I passed out with the ether. When I awakened, I remember spitting up a lot of blood because the

Schooldays: 1924–31

surgeon had cut through my swollen tonsils. However, that operation saved my life – I could once again breathe freely.

Mother nursed me until she also fell sick with diphtheria. We then had to employ a nurse to look after both of us. When I recovered I tried to take my first steps but kept falling onto the floor, as my legs felt as if they were made from jelly. I was weakened, partly due to a restricted diet, and the inability to swallow liquids, which kept coming out of my nose. This created double vision and, because I could not read myself, I had various people read books to me. It had taken longer than expected to get the strength to walk properly and it was decided eventually that I should enter the isolation ward at the General Children's Hospital. As this was a teaching hospital I was taken to a lecture theatre. I felt terribly embarrassed when made to stand naked and act as a guinea-pig for all the medical students. My last, and most horrible, memory of the hospital was the ward visit of the head of the clinic who was the renowned doctor Professor Pirquet – a world figure in chest medicine. All I received from him was the comment: 'What is this fat one doing here?' How could anyone, especially a doctor, be so insensitive to a sick child? It was one of those awful incidents that lingers in the mind.

I was extremely glad when I got home at last. The whole experience had been very traumatic for me. I had still to lie down most of the time but life was to improve. I was delighted to get a present from father of my first wireless – a crystal set with earphones. The wireless brought me constantly into the world of chamber music, for which I developed an intense liking.

By the summer of 1928 I was back to full health and went on holiday with Lotte and three friends to a Swiss *pensionat de jeunes filles* at Les Diablerets. Our three friends were Trudi, Bernhard Altmann's daughter, Lisl Bunzl who was a few years older than me and Hannerl Kerner who felt superior to all of us and showed it. Father escorted us on our overnight train journey in a third-class compartment where he made us lie on the benches, the floor and the luggage shelf. The other three girls, used to more comfort, were not too happy about the arrangement.

Those two months in the Swiss Alps provided a wonderful experience and were recorded by Lotte in many good photographs taken with her first camera, a Box Tengor. We would have learned much more French had the five of us not spoken mostly in German.

There were about 20 girls in the *pensionat* who had come from all over the world. I remember three sisters from Argentina who bemoaned the fact that they had missed the snow at home, which had fallen there for the first time in their young lives. We undertook excursions higher into the Alps from our chalets to an area of glacial brooks, cattle pastures and unique alpine flora. Up there, high in the mountains, cheese was still made in the traditional way as it had been for hundreds of years. The altitude and the climb sapped our energy which we boosted with sugar lumps with lemon juice squeezed on to them.

We always resented early lights out, and in frustration Trudi and I made up a sarcastic poem about the 'Demoiselles', the owners of the establishment. I remember having to rely on flashes of lightning to jot down the lines of our poem.

During our time there, the Swiss national holiday was celebrated. It was interesting to note that their national anthem had the same melody as the British one. There were fireworks, patriotic songs and a fancy-dress party with costumes which we made mostly from crepe paper. The party proved a great success and Lotte recorded it all with her little camera. She also won a prize for most original costume. She came as a cobbler and looked very fine with a moustache, hat, green apron and a pair of boots slung over her shoulder.

The two months passed quickly and soon it was time to

Schooldays: 1924–31

say goodbye to all the girls we had met there. Trudi's mother and brother came by car to bring us on the journey home. This was a fitting end to a lovely holiday. We stopped at Berne to see the bears in the bear pit and then went on to Zurich, where we stayed at the luxurious Hotel Dolder.

In the summers of 1930 and 1931 Lotte and I were sent for six weeks to a youth camp in Altaussee in the Salzkammergut. This is an area of beautiful scenery with a lake for swimming and woods with lots of attractive walks. We stayed in small groups of the same age in farm houses in the area but had our meals in a communal dining hall.

Although these holidays in Altaussee were enjoyable, I would have preferred to have spent them with my parents. However, at the end of our six weeks there in 1931, father and mother came to fetch Lotte and me and brought us on a family holiday. We took the train to Lienz in the east Tirol. Our hotel, across the River Drau, was at the edge of a beautiful forest. As soon as we arrived I sought permission to stroll through the woods, because I could see they were the type I loved – full of wild flowers, berries and mushrooms. I walked deep into the woods certain that I would recognise my way back to the hotel. As it got darker I realised that I had lost my way. I felt a great sense of panic which made me stop and pray. This cleared my thoughts enough to remember that we had crossed the river on arrival and thus the hotel must be in the valley. I decided to walk down to the river only to discover I had been quite close to the hotel during my walk. I never revealed my adventure to father or mother.

After two weeks there we set off by train to the south Tirol, to Dobiaco, and then by bus over the Dolomite mountains to Lake Cara. This brought us past lovely villages where most of the houses had balconies with begonias hanging down and many were decorated with large frescos, mostly depictions of saints. The roads over the high mountains had many hair-raising bends with a sheer rockface on one side and a steep precipice on the other. Our bus came face to face with a small car which was stationary in the middle of a bend. The driver of the car had been too scared to drive on and implored our driver to get the car past the dangerous spot. Our driver obliged and we all watched – he had no option if he wished to continue our journey. We spent one night at the Cara Lake Hotel which overlooks a clear blue lake surrounded by granite mountains. There was a lively dance in the hotel that evening and we were amazed to see that very young children were allowed to stay up and enjoy their games amongst the dancing couples. We noted that the Italians had a much more relaxed attitude to their young children than the straightlaced Viennese. Eventually, we took the train from Cortina, stopping in Merano and then in Bolzano. My deepest impression was of the fruit market in Bolzano with its unique fragrances of ripe fruit and the taste of the sun-drenched apricots, peaches, pears and many other fruits the likes of which I have never found anywhere else in the world. We bought some, as every traveller was allowed to import several kilos duty-free in to Austria. I am reticent about visiting Bolzano again as I fear it may not be the same today, with modern growing methods having interfered with nature – this would spoil my childhood memory.

From 1928 onwards, Lotte and I attended the Beamten Töchter Verein (Daughters of Civil Servants) Grammar School which mother had attended some 20 years previously. It still had the same director, nicknamed Rex, and several old teachers.

I had begun to dislike the school because it was so old-fashioned and was very relieved when mother decided to send me to a different grammar school for my fifth-grade year which, as it turned out, was my last year at school. Lotte changed to a commercial school at the same time. The new

Schooldays: 1924–31

school, in the city centre, was about half an hour's walk from home. It occupied the top two floors of an office building and we were taken on to the flat roof on warm summer days for our lessons. We had a good view of parts of the city centre and I remember us watching the building work on the site of the first *Hochhaus* in Vienna, a mini-skyscraper of 13 storeys. There was a happy atmosphere and I learnt more that year than in the previous years at the other grammar school. I particularly enjoyed history, art, chemistry, literature and English. I found English very easy, whereas I always had difficulties learning French. At the end of the year my class performed Oscar Wilde's *The Importance of Being Earnest*, in which I played Lady Bracknell in the first act and Cecily in the last act. The play was great fun to perform and gave us all a chance to improve our ability to speak the language.

During this school year I was allowed to take part in the school's ski course. For some years I had been keen to go on a ski course to become more proficient. It was a great sport to participate in because of the excellent facilities in Vienna. A tram ride brought us right into the ski areas of the Wienerwald, so that we could go there any time there was enough snow. The city also had two artificial open-air ice rinks which we used from time to time. I became interested in the sport after seeing Sonja Henie practise here in 1928 for the Olympics in St Moritz. She was coached by her very plump father and I remember clearly the pirouettes, the figures-of-eight and the finale of a backwards butterfly. The style was graceful and simple in contrast with the present-day intricacies of the sport. When she won an Olympic gold medal I was greatly impressed by the fact that at sixteen she was a mere four years older than I.

By 1931 our family's financial position was very difficult and there was no money for any luxuries or treats. This was a result of problems in father's business from the late 1920s. He found his brother-in-law, who had come into the business as a new associate in 1924, very difficult, and various conflicts and events caused father to lose some of the valued agencies he had started with. To compensate, he had obtained a number of Japanese agencies, but the product sales were much lower than previously. Lotte and I had then to change direction and get into situations where we could earn money as opposed to incurring school fees. From then onwards, at the ages of fourteen and fifteen respectively, Lotte and I went our separate ways.

5 · A Change of Direction: 1931–32

The next phase of my life began in the autumn of 1931 when I enrolled in the School for Catering, the Fachschule für Gastgwerbe, in the Stephansdom area, and in commerce and language classes at the Sprachschule on Wiedner Hauptstrasse. I attended catering classes each morning and the other classes in the afternoons and evenings. Although I found this a punishing schedule, I was determined to succeed and help to improve the family situation. At that point I had to give up my beloved piano lessons to save expenses.

We all played our part in helping to ease the family's financial position. Lotte had to forego her dream of becoming a professional photographer and had gone to commercial school. Father spent two-thirds of the year in Eastern Europe selling, and mother opened a small wool shop about five minutes' walk from our home.

From then on Lotte and I grew apart socially as well as in our careers. She was very interested in politics and joined socialist youth groups. These were relatively peaceful times, with no indication of the storms ahead. In 1929 the government resigned under pressure from the right and Chancellor Steeruwitz was succeeded by Schober. However, in the elections of November 1930 the socialists were totally victorious and there were no Nazis or communists elected. People involved in the socialist movements were euphoric at that time. In 1931 the only undetected warning on the horizon was the Nazi demonstration against the showing of *All Quiet on the Western Front*, the film based on Remarque's novel of the same name. At that time most Viennese Jews were liberal socialists.

I became more and more interested in literature and music. I often used my dinner money to buy concert tickets but could afford only those in the standing room section. Occasionally, I would feel faint from hunger. Aunt Joan gave me a birthday present of a subscription to a library for foreign language books. I was fond of those by John Galsworthy and read all of them.

One of our young friends, Luz Mandl, owned a bathing hut at the Old Danube, a very popular spot for swimmers. In 1932 he generously offered Lotte and me the use of the hut at any time. This was a wonderful facility for us and only a short train journey from home. During that summer we went there often on a Sunday.

One Sunday there was a new boy there. He was a schoolfriend of Luz. He seemed very nice to me and I was attracted by his slimness, his dark eyes with a dreamy expression and by his quiet manner. Later that year I met him again at a party in Luz's house. He was introduced to me and from that moment we were destined to become the centre of each other's lives. His name was Kurt and he asked to see me home. By way of conversation he declared he would never get married. At that time, at sixteen, marriage was the last thing on my mind as I was immersed in my studies. Nevertheless, from then on, we spent most of our free time together. We quickly discovered that we had similar tastes in books and in music and were both fascinated by Professor Freud's theories that many people were discussing at that time.

Kurt was twenty-five and a qualified wireless engineer when I met him. He lived with his parents in Mariahilferstrasse

A Change of Direction: 1931–32

which was about two miles from my home. His father, Lajos Sekules, and his two uncles, ran a large business producing feathers, mainly ostrich, for theatrical and evening costumes. Kurt was working as a radio technician at that time and also gave free lessons to a group of radio enthusiasts. Later, he obtained a job at the Hornyphone radio factory.

During the four years until we married in 1936 we had a wonderfully happy courtship. We usually had Sunday lunch at my future in-laws and often after I had attended some midday concert. Some seasons I bought a subscription to the Sunday midday concerts given by the Vienna Philharmonic in the Musikverein Saal on Bösendorferstrasse, not far from the Opera House. Most of these concerts left me highly elated. As I was in love I was especially receptive to such experiences. Three occasions have had a lasting impact. I remember 'walking on air' on my way to Sunday lunch after hearing Dvorak's 'Symphony No. 9 from the New World' and on another occasion after hearing Ravel's *Bolero*. Another summer Sunday at a bathing pool, I was bowled over by Brahms's 'St Anthony's Variations', which was relayed over the loudspeakers.

During the two-week summer holiday we usually backpacked in the Alps. We got to know many of the mountains but our favourites were Semmering, where the first alpine motor races were held in the 1920s, Rax and Schneeberg where the water reservoir for Vienna was located. We gathered berries and mushrooms, bought milk and eggs from local farmers and cooked our meals *al fresco* on a tiny spirit cooker. Outdoor camping was unknown to us then and so we stayed each night at an inn. In Austria one was always sure to find one at the end of the day's trek. We walked over wide areas of the mountain ranges, going from pass to pass. With our hobnailed boots and loden capes we were well protected from the frequent rain and cold. This was part of the fun. We met very few people and enjoyed the freedom to go where we pleased, as there were no barriers or restrictions. All we needed was a good map.

The catering school's curriculum expected pupils to do appropriate work during the summer break. In 1932 I found an unpaid job in a large boarding house near Vienna, on the way to Baden bei Wien, which gave me relevant experience. The work was pleasant, acting as receptionist to the guests who were from middle-class families. Some had come to convalesce, some had come before or after having a baby and others came to enjoy the country air. One day a lady guest asked me to do her a favour. She said she expected a visit from a famous person who did not want to be seen by anyone and asked me to meet the visitor and escort her to the guest's room. When the lady arrived I led her quickly to the lift and brought her up to the appropriate floor. I knew at once who the famous visitor was. It was Marlene Dietrich, who had by then become world famous because of her role in *The Blue Angel*. She was much smaller than I had imagined her. She scrutinised herself in the lift mirror and, with the famous sultry look we knew so well from her films, thanked me courteously as she left the lift. My boss was furious when she found this out after the visit because I had kept it secret. I felt it was my duty to have been discreet and the guest thanked me profusely for observing her wishes. I then found out that our guest was the famous Welsh novelist, Jean Rhys.

During the second year of the catering course we visited various related industries such as the Manner biscuit company, the Stollwerk confectionery factory, a brewery and the cellars of the vintners. That last visit was memorable. We were taken to the large cool and dark cellar and invited to sample as many varieties of wine as we wished. I drank seven glasses of various qualities but ate only one or two biscuits. When I eventually emerged into the daylight and fresh air my head spun and I was unable to walk straight. It was the first

A Change of Direction: 1931–32

time I was terribly drunk. My colleagues guided me to a nearby sports club where I rested until I was able to stagger the two miles home, always holding on to walls and railings. Next day at school we all had a good laugh at my 'disgrace'.

Older people's social life after work revolved around meetings in the coffee houses. Some evenings I joined mother at the coffee house where she regularly met friends and relatives. I was always fascinated by their wide-ranging conversations and especially when ex-soldiers described their experiences in the First World War. I was amazed that anyone could be old enough to reminisce about events that happened almost 20 years before!

In the autumn of 1932, at the start of my second year at catering school, I was extremely fortunate to get unpaid part-time work in the Hotel Bristol, one of the top hotels in Vienna. This marked the beginning of another fascinating part of my young life.

6 · The Hotel Bristol: 1932–38

In the 1930s Vienna was at the centre of the world of classical music and opera, and the Bristol was one of the world's great hotels. This combination meant that many famous people stayed in the hotel, which made it an interesting place in which to work and fascinating for anyone with a great love for music or opera.

The Bristol, together with the Grand, the Imperial and the Sacher, made up the city's great hotels and were all fairly close together, grouped around the area near the Opera House. The Bristol, situated at the corner of the Ring and Kärntnerstrasse, Vienna's exclusive shopping street, is directly opposite the Opera House. The Grand was next door, the Imperial across the Ring a few blocks east and the Sacher behind the Opera House in Philarmonikerstrasse. The Sacher, in particular, catered for the aristocracy and 'high society' and, of course, became world famous for its cake – the Sachertorte.

In the first several months I worked in the main kitchen and found that most of the chefs were reluctant to teach me anything worthwhile. For instance, I was allowed only to slice and chop vegetables when I worked in the sauce, soup and roast department. I still remember being faced with having to clean my first chicken. All through childhood I had given a wide berth to poulterers and fishmongers, displaying their

The Hotel Bristol: 1932–38

blood-soaked wares. Now I had to face up to the challenge. When the chef noticed my hesitation he shouted across 'Just grab it by the legs like this' and mimed the actions. I had to follow his instructions, succeeded in cleaning the chicken and overcame my aversion. I had more luck in the *guard-mange* – the cold kitchen. I learnt how to catch a live trout in the tank and then kill and clean it. I became adept at making the best Wiener Schnitzel, mayonnaise, salads and cold sauces. One day, as I watched the chef killing an eel by hurling it against the stone flags, I felt something cold hitting the back of my neck. I screamed, thinking it was the eel, only to find out that it was the ventilation chain which had been dislodged by the jumping eel. It was there that I first tasted frogs' legs which I found to taste like a cross between chicken and fish. I was happiest in the pâtisserie department because the chef was very willing to teach me. He was extremely inventive and I was able to collect many beautiful recipes which sadly I had little opportunity to use in later years.

The hotel, with 300 rooms and 300 staff, was more like a self-contained small town. All relevant trades and services had workshops in either the cellars or the attics and so all maintenance and repairs could be carried out in-house. There were large store rooms for linen, carpets, furnishings and furniture. The hotel had a quick-service dry cleaning department for guests and had a sewing room which carried out all hotel and guest repairs. The printshop produced all the hotel business and writing stationery and produced the daily menus in French. Technically the hotel was always up-to-date and at that time had a telephone exchange with eight lines.

Our best-known member of staff was Mr Gabriel, the head porter, who presided over his territory from behind his desk in the foyer. Everyone regarded him as a character, including the porters and bellboys who reported to him. Next desk was hotel reception, which was always staffed by men who had to wear morning suits at all times.

When my first year was completed I was accepted as a regular paid employee. We had a six-day, 60-hour working week, including mealtimes. In some departments you could be faced with late-night and weekend work which could often be strenuous. When I was off duty at night I was entitled to order a takeaway supper of cold meats. The helpings were always generous enough to share them with Kurt. These money-savers were very welcome, as our pay was low and Kurt was also expected to assist his parents financially.

Many of our guests were world-famous, and during the concert season a large proportion of them were top international musicians. This was most exciting and gave me a great opportunity to start an autograph collection which eventually comprised most of the top names in the musical world at that time. These included such famous artists as Fyodor Chaliapin and Arturo Toscanini. I bought a leather-bound album especially for the purpose. My favourite musicians were, of course, the pianists and I succeeded in getting autographs of many of them such as Rachmaninov, Horowitz, Backhaus and Alfred Cortot. I was also lucky enough to get Yehudi Menuhin's autograph and a signed photograph of the singer Richard Tauber.

Bruno Walter, who always stayed at the Bristol, was by then regarded as one of the world's great conductors. I remember clearly meeting him in the foyer, where he agreed to sign my autograph book.

I had gone to attend a lecture in the Konzerthaus Concert Hall on the occasion of Sigmund Freud's 80th birthday in 1936. Freud was not present due to illness. The guest speaker was Thomas Mann, by then one of the giants of world literature and a Nobel prizewinner. He was of medium height and had piercing dark eyes. He spoke freely about Freud's achievements and their impact on the thinking of the time. He had a pronounced north German accent which sounded very different from the way we spoke German in Vienna.

The Hotel Bristol: 1932–38

After the lecture I went to the artist's room where many personalities were milling around having a celebratory buffet. I again met Bruno Walter there who brought me to meet the famous author and so I obtained my precious autograph. On the way home I reflected on the coincidence of meeting Thomas Mann and previously Marlene Dietrich who had been made famous as a result of his brother Heinrich's writing.

In January 1933 an advertisement in a travel agency attracted my attention. It offered a weekend at the Munich Carnival at a price I thought that I could afford. Firstly, I organised a switch of my day off so that I would be free for the two consecutive days and then persuaded Aunt Joan to join me in the venture.

We set off from Vienna on the evening train and arrived in Munich about midnight. We stayed there in a hotel and next morning took another train, on which they served breakfast first-class, to the well-known winter sports-resort of Garmisch. At Garmisch we met an elderly uncle and aunt who were holidaying there. They brought us by automobile to their hotel and then on a sleigh-ride to a local beauty spot and finally to a ski-jumping display. Then came one of those moments you can never forget – my first flight. Aunt Joan and I were treated to a flight in a tiny plane which took off from a frozen lake and flew around the famous Zugspitze mountain. As the weather was sunny and the sky crystal clear we got our first spectacular views of the snowclad Alps.

We returned to Munich that evening to attend a political cabaret which was full of material against the rising Nazis. The audience, whom I assumed were mainly anti-Nazi, was in a carnival mood and thoroughly enjoyed all the satirical jokes. As this was a few weeks prior to the Nazi election victory in Germany, Munich was plastered with posters and bunting, which promoted the National Socialist Party.

Surviving the Nazis, Exile and Siberia

Our trip to Munich had been very enjoyable and, even with the political atmosphere, we didn't get any inkling of the problems that lay ahead. The year 1933 was to be one of turbulence and change in Germany which, in turn, affected Austrian life. After their victory, the Nazi government started its anti-Semitic campaign at once by banning 'Ayrian'–Jewish marriages and introduced sterilisation of certain categories of citizens. Generally in Austria the sentiments were anti-Nazi, with Chancellor Dollfus banning Nazi meetings, sending many Nazis to concentration camps and finally banning all Nazi organisations. Tension increased through the summer as Hitler closed the Austrian border to non-Nazis, and was fuelled by press articles revealing a Nazi plan to invade Austria. The Jewish situation in Germany deteriorated quickly with confirmation of Jews being sent to concentration camps and by the exodus of Jewish artists, such as Otto Klemperer, Bertolt Brecht, Walter Gropius and Paul Klee. In September, Dollfuss became dictator after his cabinet resigned and he declared that 'democracy is dead'. A month later he was shot by a Nazi assassin but was able to continue in office. Martial law was declared in November and the Nazi leader, Frauenfeld, arrested. Although some Jews were leaving Austria amid this scene of changing turmoil, it was not yet evident to us how perilous the situation would become eventually for all Jews in Austria.

The tensions continued and worsened in early 1934. Although the Chancellor was anti-Nazi, his 'Fatherland Front' was seen as a pernicious fascist organisation which backed up his dictatorial tendencies. In February the Social Democrats came on to the streets of Vienna and a major uprising ensued. The uprising was brutally crushed by Dollfuss with hundreds killed and wounded by army machine guns and mortars. I remember this uprising clearly as I happened to be on late evening restaurant duty and had to stay in the hotel overnight as it was too dangerous to go home. When I awoke in the morning I heard the gunfire as the army were now

The Hotel Bristol: 1932–38

firing on the workers' apartments. The uprising created a state of emergency during which hundreds of Social Democrats, including Mayor Seitz, were sent to prison or to concentration camps. All Dollfuss's supporters wore fascist (Heimwehr) uniforms and used brutal methods against all opposition. Dollfuss was officially confirmed dictator in April and all opposition parties abolished. That was the end of socialism and democracy in Austria for many years. Ironically, Dollfuss was assassinated by the Nazis three months later which caused many Nazi arrests and Italy's offer to help.

We read of the worsening position of Jews in Germany all through 1935 and of the tensions in Austria. In April, plans were announced to boost the Austrian army and introduce conscription, in violation of the peace treaties of the First World War. Later that month, in Germany, Hitler banned all non-Aryans from any type of literary work and went further in August by banning all marriages between Jews and non-Jews. Finally, in September, all Jews were deprived of German citizenship and excluded from a whole range of activities including public life, teaching, journalism, farming, radio, theatre and films.This did not soften our worries of possible anti-Semitism in our own fascist organisation. It was still 'wait and see' for Austrian Jews as the year drew to a close.

The following year, 1936, was far more significant for me and full of important memories. On the political and military fronts, turmoil remained. Military service was introduced, in contravention of the peace treaties, and troops were sent to the German border at the end of April, as an invasion by Hitler was feared. Chancellor von Schuschnigg, successor to Dollfuss, became head of the 'Fatherland Front', absorbed the fascist Heimwehr into it and became dictator. In July he got Hitler to declare that Germany recognised Austrian independence. Throughout all this turbulence I had two wonderfully happy events – a marathon weekend in the summer at the Salzburg music festival and my marriage in November.

Surviving the Nazis, Exile and Siberia

I went alone to the Salzburg music festival so that I could be totally free to choose performances and not impose my choice on anyone else. In the two days, I attended a number of concerts, a play and an opera and had time for lots of sightseeing. The first of these concerts was a piano recital by the one-armed pianist Wittgenstein. He was a brother of the famous philosopher and had lost an arm in the Great War. At that concert I bumped into an old school friend who had come to the festival with her brother and their parents. This meeting was to turn out particularly lucky for me. The second was a concert of chamber music. I then attended a recital of a Mozart mass in the Dome and my final visit was to the Marionetten Theatre to see and hear a brilliant performance of *The Magic Flute*.

In the Domplatz I saw an open-air play directed by Max Reinhard. The play was *Jederman*, a morality piece by Hoffmannsthal and, at one point, the voice of 'God' boomed out from the castle on the mountain overlooking the square. Reinhard, one of the initiators of the festival, had to flee to the United States in 1938.

I was very lucky with the main opera performance. I knew that all tickets were sold out and anyhow I could not have afforded one. I had just gone to the Festival House to watch the arrival of all the elegant people when, suddenly, the brother of my schoolfriend, whom I'd met earlier in the Mozarteum, approached and said, 'Do you want to come in?'. I was absolutely delighted and we were admitted after he had shown two tickets on entry to the theatre. Inside, he said 'You can safely stand here behind the back row, as no one will bother you.' Thus I was able to enjoy the whole stunning performance of my favourite opera, *Fidelio*, conducted by mæstro Toscanini.

Kurt and I were married on 2 November 1936. We both had planned a very simple wedding and took the view that it was

The Hotel Bristol: 1932–38

our own private affair. It was a cold rainy day and I shivered from a mixture of the weather, hunger and excitement. Adhering to tradition, I did not see my bridegroom nor did I eat before the ceremony. I wore a royal blue silk dress with a matching hat which was meant to resemble a coronet. At that time everyone was excitedly looking forward to the coronation of Edward VIII in London and so I thought the hat's style appropriate. Unknown to us, mother had invited all the extended families and we were surprised at the large crowd present at the synagogue and later at our home. Aunt Lily had prepared an extensive buffet and I was pleased with all the fuss and especially with lots of beautiful and useful presents.

There could not have been a greater contrast between our wedding and that of my parents 22 years before, in 1914. There was no trousseau, no dowry, no apartment of our own with custom-built furniture and, of course, no honeymoon on the Adriatic. In fact we had no honeymoon because we risked losing our jobs by asking for the time off and, apart from that, we could not have afforded it. We were delighted to be able to live with my parents, as Lotte generously agreed to move into the tiny unused maid's room so that we could rearrange our former nursery into a bedsitter. We lived there for the rest of our pre-war days in Vienna.

The year 1937 was less eventful politically at the beginning although the position of Jews in Germany was getting ever more perilous. It proved, yet again, an interesting and exciting year to work at the Hotel Bristol. One of the big events of the year was the controversial visit of the Duke and Duchess of Windsor to Berlin in October to be fêted by the Nazi hierarchy. Some weeks prior to the visit they were guests in our hotel. They occupied the royal suite with its sumptuous bathroom in white and yellow marble and gold-plated fittings. I remember clearly how strikingly elegant the Duchess

Surviving the Nazis, Exile and Siberia

looked, and more regal than the Duke. Their room-service bill showed a high consumption of whisky.

We had one very eccentric guest, Mr Blumenthal, at that time. When I started at the hotel, he already had been there many years and was only to leave in mid-1938 when the Nazi annexation forced him to flee to Switzerland. He was very rich and highly intelligent but his life was ruled by many taboos. He was so afraid of contamination that he wore white gloves by day and by night, changing them several times daily. He changed shirts so often that the hotel assigned him his own full-time washerwoman. When he received letters someone would spread them on the table to enable him to read them without touching them. Many years later, when I read of this type of behaviour by the American millionaire Howard Hughes, I kept thinking of Mr Blumenthal. In all the years I worked in the hotel I met him only once, by chance, in a corridor. He was very small with a pale complexion which contrasted with his piercing black eyes. I thought 'Poor little rich man!'

Another celebrity guest was an Indian maharajah who arrived with his large retinue which included his two personal cooks with their metal trunks filled with Indian spices and ingredients. They were allocated space in the kitchens to prepare all their special meals. The maharani unfortunately suffered from a disease which made her fall asleep, unless she was entertained constantly by a lady companion.

I was to work in the Hotel Bristol for six years, and to serve in many departments, often as holiday replacement. During the summer I usually 'stood in' in many different departments such as telephone exchange, printing workshop, control office, restaurant cash desk and chief housekeeper (*Gouvernante*). Whilst I worked at the Bristol Lotte helped mother in her wool shop and developed her own social life. She joined an alpine club and spent her weekends hiking, rock-climbing, swimming or sailing, depending on the season.

The Hotel Bristol: 1932–38

Among Lotte's climbing and hiking friends was one called Vicky. An Auschwitz survivor, he became the famous doctor and philosopher Victor Frankl. Another friend, Richard Hauser (Ricky) survived the war in Australia and became well known as a social reformer. In the post-war years he lived in London and married Yehudi Menuhin's sister, Hephzibah.

All through 1937 the political situation in Austria grew very tense and we could almost feel the Nazi menace looming on the German border. Early 1938 saw things become much worse. In January Romania's announcement that they intended to expel 500,000 Jews sent a shudder of fear through us all. In February Hitler started to put the pressure on Austria by asking Chancellor Schuschnigg to free Nazis and appoint pro-Nazi ministers and then demanding the right of self-determination for Germans in both Austria and Czechoslovakia. Knowing what had happened in Germany since 1933 we felt extremely apprehensive. The Chancellor's broadcast telling Jews that they had nothing to fear had the opposite effect to what was intended. A few short weeks later, Hitler drove victoriously into Vienna to a tumultuous reception and was the honoured guest at the Hotel Imperial.

The events of late 1937 and early 1938 did not prevent me from attending two or three concert or opera performances every week. It was always standing room, to fit into my limited budget. Ironically, father teased me by saying 'You are living as if the world is coming to an end'. Little did he know how prophetic this comment was. I attended the opera for the last time in January 1938. It was a performance of Wagner's *Tristan and Isolde*, which was ruined by a stink bomb thrown into the auditorium in protest at the conductor Bruno Walter, because he was Jewish. After the effect of the bomb subsided, the show went ahead without singing because the soprano was too distressed to sing and so just acted her part.

My world was indeed about to come to an end very soon.

Surviving the Nazis, Exile and Siberia

In early 1938 I commented to a colleague that I thought it was time to look for another country. She replied 'Don't be silly. You were born and bred here; you have nothing to fear.' Later, when I found out that her son was an illegal Nazi, I felt that the net must be closing in. By late February we had decided to try to emigrate and so I appealed to the hotel president for a pay rise and justified this by claiming I would need more money to emigrate. He, too, told me I was talking nonsense.

March 1938 became the pivotal month in our lives. On the 11th, we were all glued to our radios to hear Chancellor Schuschnigg's abdication speech, which sent a shiver down our backs. We knew that normal life had ended for us Jews. The Nazis were consolidating their grip on the country and on the same day German troops invaded Austria at the request of the new pro-Nazi Chancellor, Arthur Seyss-Inquart, who had succeeded Schuschnigg. Within two days the Reunification Act recognised the *'Anschluss'* – the annexation of the country by Germany. The next day Hitler drove through Vienna in triumph amidst scenes of tumultuous enthusiasm, which indicated clearly the depth of support for him and for the Nazi cause. It was my day off and I was at home. When I saw the squadrons of German aircraft with the swastika markings, I knew our hour of doom had come. Although strictly forbidden, Kurt's family were able to watch Hitler's cavalcade from their apartment balcony because the Mariahilferstrasse was on the direct route from the Westbahnhof, where he arrived, to his destination – the Hotel Imperial on the Ringstrasse. Church bells were pealing to welcome the German dictator who had just made the country a mere province of the Reich. The cavalcade was headed by tanks followed by fieldguns and Hitler went past standing up in his open car and wearing the brown uniform of his Storm Troopers. He gave the fascist salute to the wildly cheering crowds watching from every vantage point. Many

The Hotel Bristol: 1932–38

Nazi supporters came from as far away as Czechoslovakia. Several people wept with joy, young girls threw flowers and the Young Nazis kept screaming 'We want to see our Führer'. The cavalcade arrived at the Hotel Imperial at around six in the evening. The hotel had been requisitioned for Hitler and his entourage and all guests had been sent away. He then appeared on the hotel balcony and took the salute as the Austrian and German troops marched down the Ringstrasse. The crowd kept cheering and asking him to stay on the balcony. The welcome was unprecedented, even for the Hapsburg emperors. There would never be any doubt again that Austria was a deeply fascist country.

As with all the Nazi takeovers, things moved forward at alarming speed. When I turned up for work at the Bristol the following morning one of the directors told me I no longer had a job and sent me home with a note which stated: 'Dismissed – reason Jewish'. Although I should have suspected the inevitable, it was nevertheless a terrible blow and it didn't help that I was then seven months pregnant with our first child. It transpired that about half the staff of the hotel had been illegal members of the National Socialist Party for some time and were organised to get rid of certain people. They took over all the important jobs immediately and made sure that our hotel president and a Jewish director were both sent to prison.

7 · The Second Goodbye: 1938

On 18 March, four days after Hitler's triumphant entry to Vienna, the pogrom commenced. The Nazi press called it 'the great spring-cleaning'. Jews were excluded from professions, Jewish judges dismissed, Jewish shops had to put notices up to identify themselves. Theatres and concert halls were 'cleansed' of Jewish artists, conductors and directors. Three weeks later the Nazis started to send prominent Jews to Dachau concentration camp and seized Rothschild's Bank, arresting Baron Rothschild.

Our family situation disintegrated very quickly. Shortly after I lost my job, Kurt lost his. Father could not get any business even from long-standing customers and mother's wool shop was taken over by a Nazi commissar, without any compensation paid. We had all lost our income. All we could do to survive was to let some of the rooms in our apartment and sell the piano and other luxuries. As we were desperate for money, I decided to go to the Labour Court and try to claim redundancy pay.

My first child, Ruth, was born on 4 May 1938. I felt so delighted and proud to be a mother. Luckily, my health insurance as a former employee held good, and I went to a hospital staffed by Catholic nuns, where I was in very good hands. It was an island of peace and sanity in a world of indignity and persecution of Jews.

The Second Goodbye: 1938

The Nazi grip on the country was total and, with typical German efficiency, the whole life of the state was taken over. To justify the annexation, a plebiscite was held throughout Austria and Germany on 10 April. Of course, it would have required suicidal courage to vote 'No' in a polling room filled with Storm Troopers. After voting 'Yes', voters were decorated with a gilt badge showing Hitler's head surrounded by the slogan, 'One people. One Reich. One Führer'. To add credence to the process, much was made of the fact that Cardinal Innitzer of Vienna voted in favour. He was one of the first to cast a vote and gave the Nazi salute as he entered and left the polling station and proudly wore his 'One Führer' badge. Almost 100 per cent voted 'Yes'. Jews were forbidden to vote and threatened with severe penalties if they tried to.

Hitler then had 'approval' for his actions and proceeded to tighten the noose around the Jewish population even further. From June all Austrians had to prove Aryan ancestry to be allowed to marry and by the end of June employers had to give all Jewish employees 14 days notice of dismissal. Shortly after this, Jewish suicides became common in the city.

We proceeded to try to get out of the country as soon as we could. Kurt and I wrote dozens of letters to radio factories abroad to find him a job as a wireless engineer. We also applied for an immigration permit into Australia. We would have gone to England as domestic servants but did not qualify because we had our baby daughter. Luckily Lotte qualified for nursing training in England and got away.

The situation got more and more menacing for Jews as summer progressed. It always felt more depressing when the weather was beautiful and forced you to contrast with happier times. There were daily arrests, damage to Jewish shops and other restrictions. Jews were banned from sitting on the benches on the Ringstrasse and from entering any public park. To give baby Ruth fresh air and sunshine I had to wheel her pram to a private allotment, about one hour's walk from our home.

We still had a daily help. I got her to show me how to launder as, until then, I'd only washed sweaters and gloves. I also practised dressmaking by taking my maternity dress to pieces and then sewing it into an ordinary dress. I knew this would be a necessary skill if we ended up in the wilds somewhere. I wore my 'new' dress for many years. Kurt got a job teaching his speciality at a vocational training school. There was a big demand for vocational training because doctors, lawyers and business people wished to retrain in a practical trade suitable for emigration.

The Labour Court hearing on my redundancy claim had been set for the middle of June. On the morning of the hearing the door bell rang at seven o'clock. The Gestapo had arrived to escort me to their headquarters for interrogation. These were in the Hotel Metropole at Franz-Josefs Kai on the Danube Canal. They allowed me to bring my six-week-old baby with me.

I was taken to an empty office. Soon a man in civilian clothes arrived and began his interrogation. To my astonishment I was accused of being a communist and it was alleged that my former colleagues had refused to work with me. Consequently I had had to be sacked without any further pay. He did declare his surprise at being faced by someone who was only twenty-two – he had expected a much older and worldly-wise harridan. He then stopped and telephoned the Hotel Bristol to demand witnesses to attend his office at once. I could tell from the tone of the conversation that there was panic and unease at the other end of the line. I presumed the Gestapo had that effect on most people.

When the baby became hungry she started yelling at the top of her voice. I was shown to a hotel room so that I could feed her. When I came out of that room I was faced by my

The Second Goodbye: 1938

former work-mates. They wanted to talk to me but I turned away – I was furious because I assumed that they had landed me in this serious trouble with the Gestapo.

After the witnesses had been interrogated I was summoned back to the office. My interrogator said at once, 'I am submitting your case to my superior. You wait here.' My short wait alone in that office seemed an eternity. However, when he returned, my interrogator had a thin smile on his face. He said, 'You're a very lucky young woman. Most people in your situation would be on their way to the concentration camp at Dachau but you may go home now!' Obviously some of my work colleagues had been forced to tell the truth about me and this was accepted. I was so relieved that I sprinted down the stairs, with Ruth in my arms, and when I got on to the street Kurt was waiting. As soon as I relayed my good news he made his way as quickly as possible to the Labour Court, where my case was in progress. When he arrived he heard the prosecuting counsel declare 'This woman is on her way to Dachau by now.' After Kurt informed our lawyer that I had been freed by the Gestapo the court was informed and the case postponed. A few days later a telephone call from the Hotel offered a 50 per cent out-of-court settlement. Naturally we gladly accepted this as it would give us a chance to pay for our hoped-for emigration.

Father, mother, Kurt, baby and I were then all living together in two rooms of our apartment. The other three were let out and had to be rented to Jewish tenants. My parents enjoyed their first grandchild and were very involved in, and delighted with, her development. As we knew we would not be together for much longer we had professional photographs taken of all of us.

We spent a lot of time queuing at a number of offices to obtain all the various documents prescribed for emigration, even though we did not yet know where to go. Always, there were rumours about many possible destinations and that visas could be bought for many of the South American countries. However, we found out that Estonia was the only country which admitted tourists without a visa.

In August we received two replies from Estonian radio factories to Kurt's job applications. Although the replies were cautious, but not negative, they gave us some hope. The situation in Vienna was getting ever more tense, and by now no Jewish family had escaped some form of suffering or worse. Generally the political and military scene throughout Europe looked very menacing and many thought war to be inevitable. Some time after Lotte emigrated to England we held a big family gathering to seek their advice. All agreed that Kurt should leave as quickly as possible before he might be arrested like so many others. I asked him, 'Do you wish to leave alone or shall Ruth and I go with you?' He was adamant that the three of us should stay together.

The obvious way to get to Estonia was to go by air and so the next day we bought return tickets to Tallinn. Luggage restrictions in those days gave each passenger a very limited amount. We packed the little we were allowed to take on the plane into two suitcases and had the baby basket filled with Ruth's layette. We bade an excited farewell to all the relations who came to Schwechat airport to see us off. We then had to undergo a thorough body and luggage search. Even the baby was stripped in case we were attempting to smuggle valuables or money in excess of the ten D-Marks allowed to each person. We were slightly apprehensive as we boarded the plane – it was our first airline flight.

We flew out on 28 September 1938, the same day that Prime Minister Neville Chamberlain left London to meet Hitler at the four-power peace conference in Munich. The first leg of our flight was to Berlin, where we stayed in a good hotel. Next day we continued our flight, touching down at Königsberg (Kaliningrad), Danzig (Gdansk), Kovno (Kaunas)

The Second Goodbye: 1938

and Riga before arriving in Tallinn late that evening. At Kovno a customs official took our passports and went away to an office. We panicked momentarily, thinking that we would never see the passports again and that we would be marooned in Lithuania without any documents. However, all ended well – it was a routine check. We continued the journey to Tallinn and looked forward on arrival to meeting the director of the radio factory. We had sent a telegram advising him of our journey.

8 · Reflections on Vienna

Just to live in Vienna had been a constant joy to me. In later years I would often contemplate on my luck at having spent my childhood and youth there. Of course, the period prior to 1934 was especially memorable. The Social Democratic government was in power and generated a tremendous atmosphere of optimism. Vienna was a vibrant city where everyone assumed a bright future, even though times were financially tough for many of us. The government made great strides in meeting the needs of the people. Model blocks of workers' apartments were built; the school system became very good and the facilities for sports and recreation were impressive. The most popular sports were skating, swimming and football (for boys). There were so many beautiful parks that everyone used for games and for strolling.

The great added attraction for me was the fact that Vienna was an artistic and musical treasure-trove. As the capital of the musical world, it provided opportunities to see and hear the best performers. At a pinch I could afford quite a lot of these unique offerings and so over the years paid many visits to the theatres, the concerts and the opera. At weekends I could visit a wide range of museums and exhibitions.

After I began work in 1932 at the Hotel Bristol, I gained a new set of experiences. I walked between home and the hotel each day. If I got up early enough, I had time to meet a friend for a quick breakfast in a coffee shop and then stroll through the parks on the Ringstrasse to the hotel which was opposite the Opera House. Another option was to walk through the centre of the Old City past the impressive Michäler Tor in the Hofburg complex, buy some fruit on the way and walk on to the hotel via the Josefsplatz, the very elegant square with the famous Spanish Riding School, the Court Library and Palffy and Pallavicini palaces. During my lunch-hour I often strolled down Kärntnerstrasse, Vienna's Bond Street, to the Graben and admired all the shop windows. I felt I would never afford the expensive china, crystalware, designer clothes and shoes but I loved to look and dream. I also often browsed through the elegant art and book shops along the way.

During weekends in spring and autumn we often took a tram-ride and then walked up the gentle slopes of the Wiener Wald to find a little inn. Here, we would enjoy a *Kracherl* (fizzy lemonade) or a glass of redcurrant wine with our packed lunches whilst admiring the view of the city spread out along the Danube. In winter we could enjoy a few hours skiing from which we returned home exhausted but exhila-rated. In summer we went to the three *Strandbäder* (beaches) along the Danube and spent many hours swimming. There were numerous cafés where the elderly sat and where we all could meet in the event of bad weather. As children, we loved the illustrated magazines which circulated freely, whilst the grown-ups chatted away.

It was a life of pleasure and fulfilment, in spite of our meagre incomes. We could enjoy outings for little money, because of excellent public transport, and by eating packed lunches.

I realise that you tend to reminisce through rose-tinted spectacles when your life is shattered for ever. However, looking back over all these years, I remember mainly the joyous occasions during my first 22 years.

Part 2

Exile: 1938–47

9 · Estonia:
September 1938–June 1941

The Estonian authorities admitted us as tourists. As we were clearing our luggage a lady approached us and introduced herself. Shortly after that the director of the radio factory approached us, introduced himself and agreed to meet Kurt the next day. There were no fewer than three cars at the airport waiting to take us into Tallinn! It was all quite bewildering and confusing.

The lady was Mrs Itskovits, president of the Women's Zionist Organisation in Tallinn. After she introduced herself she took baby Ruth in her arms and held her all through the journey to our hotel in the city. Luckily, she spoke excellent German and explained how she and the others at the airport knew of our arrival and of our background. The Chief Rabbi in Tallinn had received a telegram from our worried relatives in Vienna stating, 'Woman and baby arriving. Please help when landed.' The Rabbi notified her and she mobilised two friends with cars to meet us. The plan, in case of any difficulties, was that Mrs Itskovits would hold on to the baby and the Red Cross would claim the mother. Luckily there was no need to put the plan into effect.

We were the first Jewish refugees to arrive in Tallinn. No one could foresee how the authorities would react. We arrived with return air tickets and were admitted as genuine tourists, allowed to stay for three months. Consequently the

Surviving the Nazis, Exile and Siberia

strategy set up by Mrs Itskovits wasn't needed. However, the telegram from Vienna put us in touch with the right people from the start.

In 1938 Estonia was a democracy, headed by the much-loved President Paets. The country had been independent from the Soviet Union since 1920. The original population were Estonians with their own language which is akin to Finnish and Hungarian. After centuries of German occupation there remained a large German-speaking population with its own schools and its religious and cultural institutions. Then followed a Russian occupation, which again left behind another group, with its own language, schools and institutions. The fourth group was made up of Jews, most of whom had fled from the Russian pogroms at the start of the century. Again, they had their schools, clubs, religious and cultural institutions. These Jews had never forgotten what it was like to be persecuted and become refugees. Hence, they extended every possible help and kindness to us. At that time the different groups appeared to live peacefully side by side, particularly in the small capital city.

Next day, in the lobby of the hotel, we met another refugee. We listened to the hotel radio and were just in time to hear Neville Chamberlain declare 'I believe it is peace in our time.' When Kurt went to comment, I stopped him at once. What if the other 'refugee' was a Gestapo spy? I was getting paranoid and still felt the intimidation of our recent life in Vienna under the Nazis. As it happened, the man turned out to be another hunted refugee like ourselves.

Kurt was not accepted by the radio factory, which was the largest in Tallinn. However, our new-found friends put us quickly in touch with important citizens and as a result, Kurt obtained a job within a week in a small radio factory. The staff comprised the working owners and about 20 employees. They

Estonia: September 1938–June 1941

produced high-quality radios and Kurt soon fitted in well. He had no communication problems because, luckily, the owner was highly educated and fluent in German as well as Russian and his native Estonian.

The next Viennese family to arrive consisted of an elderly lady and her two grown-up sons. The elder son set about learning the Estonian language and acquired a working knowledge in less than three months. This impressed the authorities so much that they granted the family a year's visa. We, however, had to continue to apply every three months for an extension. This was forthcoming because Kurt was in full-time employment.

Mrs Itskovits had decided that we shouldn't attract the attention of the Tallinn police and felt it would be safer for us to live in the country. She had arranged rent-free accommodation for us in a friend's house in a country village some miles outside the city. After a short train journey we arrived at our new home. It was a typical Russian *datcha* which had been used each summer by the owner but was now let out. There were other tenants, all local people.

We were immediately accepted by our neighbours, who proved very helpful in the months ahead. We had the use of one large room where we cooked, ate, slept and did our laundry. Water came from a well in the garden which had a bucket attached to a strong chain. All my cooking had to be done on a primus stove, lent to me by a neighbour. The fuel was petroleum but required methylated spirits to ignite the proper flame. I never took to the stove as I could never work it efficiently. All water was boiled on it and my food often boiled over or got burnt. I just had to grin and bear it because nappies had to be washed, the baby needed to be bathed and Kurt needed a warm supper when he came home from work.

When I went shopping in the village store for the first time I had two wonderful surprises. I had worried about language

Surviving the Nazis, Exile and Siberia

problems, but discovered that the shop owner was a *Balten-Deutsche* (the term used for a German who had lived in Estonia all his life but had not taken Soviet nationality) and so there was immediate communication. The second surprise came when I discovered the price of food. At first I was shocked at the egg price which I assumed was for a single egg. In fact, it was the price for a dozen. It turned out that the food in Estonia was incredibly cheap, very plentiful and of the highest quality. Sour cream was so rich and thick that it could be carried home in paper, like butter. In the Tallinn market there was plenty of poultry, a wide variety of fresh fish and a great range of fruit and vegetables. At the end of each working week Kurt visited the market and bought a chicken and other items. We could live a modest and healthy life on his pay.

From the earliest days in the village our social life centred around visits from city friends of Mrs Itskovits and we quickly made friends with many of our neighbours. When they found out I was a good hand-knitter I got a number of commissions which allowed me to earn a little whilst I looked after Ruth. I remember clearly spending many weeks knitting a full-length dress of fine yarn which proved very difficult but gave me confidence and experience, which were useful in later years.

To maintain contact with relatives and friends, who were now scattered over several countries, we wrote frequent letters. We always made copies whether they were written by hand or produced by whoever had access to a typewriter, because we sent them to different addresses. Until early 1939 most of both our families still lived in Vienna and had to suffer the results of the infamous 'Kristall Nacht' in November 1938, when all the synagogues in the city were set on fire and all Jewish shops destroyed. Lotte, Aunt Frieda, her daughter Gerti and son-in-law Karl were the only near relatives who had emigrated at that time and all of them had settled in London.

Estonia: September 1938–June 1941

A few weeks after settling in Estonia, we sent back our unused return flight tickets which enabled father to get a refund. This was a help in defraying the huge expenses he incurred by sending us a number of very large parcels by post. He even posted the pram, in dismantled form, which proved a real godsend. Father was especially diligent at keeping us up-to-date about who had left and about all current addresses and other details. However, as all letters were censored, the content had to be strictly personal, so that we never had any comments about 'Kristall Nacht' or other political events in Vienna. Lotte was also a faithful letter-writer and would send lovely little garments for Ruth, which she had personalised by embroidering a flower or a monogram.

Lotte managed to find mother a job as a cook in London and so she qualified for a visa. Mother left Vienna in February 1939 and was never to see my father again. Father and grandmother had no chance of a visa then and had to remain. They both died a few months apart in the following year – father from the effects of malnutrition and tuberculosis; grandmother from starvation and old age. I've always imagined that my parents' parting must have been extremely painful, because they both fully appreciated how bad things had become for Jews in the city. Mother never would talk about it in later years.

Mother started life in London as cook for a household with a little girl, her mother and her grandmother. Mother felt sorry for the little girl because she was forced to play alone in the house all day. Eventually, mother took the child with her when shopping to cheer her up. This led to a confrontation with the child's mother who rebuked mother for her cheek in taking the child away from the house. Thereafter, the atmosphere was, at best, businesslike.

Kurt's parents, his brother and his brother's wife left Vienna in spring 1939 to start a new life in Northern Ireland. This was to prove fateful for us and to shape the major part of

Surviving the Nazis, Exile and Siberia

our lives. They had obtained visas under a British government scheme to establish new business in the province. They started a factory in Londonderry with a local partner to manufacture artificial flowers, a similar operation to their former business in Vienna.

Later in 1939 my mother's brother Fritz and wife Lily and her parents moved to France and then to England. They lived for most of the war in Bedford, but their wartime experience was blighted by the internment of my uncle and my cousin in a camp on the Isle of Man. This contributed to my uncle's untimely death in 1943.

Gradually the letters dried up. Every day I would ask my neighbours *Kiri?* (any letters?) in my best Estonian. Generally the answer was *Ei ole* (none), to my great disappointment. Most of what I found out about our family was learnt only after the war was long over.

Life had to go on, however, and we had to make the best of things. We missed our families very much and, at times, reminisced in great detail to counteract our loneliness and sadness. I missed the cultural and work activities that had made Vienna so vibrant for me when growing up. We both had urban upbringings and close intense family ties. Now we had to adjust to rural conditions in a strange country. It was difficult, but was made easier by the help we got from everyone. It was to prepare us for much more difficult times ahead. Of course, there were many good times, but they were always clouded by the uncertainty that there would be no end or no returning. The uncertainty ate into the mind as the weeks progressed with nothing hopeful on the horizon.

The highlight of our existence at this time was our weekly visit to Mrs Itskovits in Tallinn. We had a standing invitation for Saturday lunch. The family owned a large apartment building which had been completed shortly before we came to Estonia. The Itskovits were wealthy business people whose

Estonia: September 1938–June 1941

factory produced a range of curtains and household textiles. The husband, son Isi and daughter Berta all worked in the business. We were most impressed as this was the first time we had seen a private apartment with central heating, constant hot water and an electric cooker. In Vienna we had heated with coke and cooked with gas. Mrs Itskovit's mother and two sons lived in the apartment, and Berta, their married daughter, had her own apartment in the house. There was always a full table and lively conversation each Saturday.

At lunch, they all spoke in German to help us understand but, as the conversations developed, some would inevitably lapse into Russian or Estonian or Yiddish. We had difficulty with these and, although we could understand Yiddish, we couldn't speak it. The food was kosher but typically Russian. Popular dishes were *borsht* (beetroot soup), *pirogen* (meat-filled pastry) and *zimmes* (meat with prune and apple stew). As the pudding had to be free of milk or cream, we had either stewed fruit or *Rosa Manna*, a fluffy creamy concoction of semolina and fruit juice. I can still imagine the taste of all of these, the culinary highlight of our week.

Another advantage of these visits was our ability to get foreign news. There was an excellent radio in the apartment which was tuned mostly to BBC News. It was from these bulletins that we learnt of the death of Sigmund Freud and of the landing in Scotland of Rudolf Hess. Sometimes we danced to the *Lambeth Walk* or *Violetta*, or other hits of the time.

I had yet to experience the Estonian winter. October and November 1938 passed without incident as the weather was still mild. All changed in December. We had strong winds, deep and driving snow and ice everywhere. My bucket would freeze to the rim of the well; the washing would go stiff on the line; the room was very cold, mainly because I didn't know how to light a woodfire in the large tiled stove. When Ruth cried almost continuously from the severe cold, I had to abandon my principle of not sleeping with the child and brought her into our bed to keep her warm with my body heat. The last straw was when the water froze indoors in the jug. I had had enough of life in the country. I took the train into Tallinn and looked for lodgings.

We found a furnished room in the very centre of the city. There was barely room for the two beds, wardrobe, baby's basket, table and two chairs but it was all that we could afford. As I was allowed into the kitchen only to fetch water, I had to cook on my primus stove on the deep sill of the window in our room, which caused the landlady to worry that I might ruin the curtains. As we had no access to a yard, we had to cook, eat, sleep, launder and dry the washing in our tiny room. But there were compensations. We were near Kurt's place of work and nearby was an eating house which served inexpensive tasty hot meals. Kurt loved to eat there. His favourite dishes became the bouillon with chunks of beef in it and, for pudding, whipped cream topped with jam.

I began to adjust gradually to the severity of the winter but was once almost caught out badly. I had to go out in freezing weather with a sharp biting wind. Not far from our lodgings, a man stopped me, kept pointing at his nose and shouting *'Nina valge!'* This meant 'white nose' and so he was warning me that I was about to suffer frostbite. I rushed home and held my nose under a cold tap. Luckily I was in time to avoid any lasting damage.

I saw the 1939 New Year in at the ball in the Jewish Club, as guest of the Itskovits. As president of WIZO (the Women's Zionist Organisation), Mrs Itskovits was very public-spirited and involved in many activities of the Jewish community, whilst her husband concentrated all his energies on the business. The ball was one of the highlights of her year and I felt honoured to be her guest. Kurt didn't object to his babysitting activities. The evening turned out to be a glittering affair and I was delighted that I had optimistically

Estonia: September 1938–June 1941

packed my one and only evening dress when we left Vienna. I travelled to and from the ball in a hired horse-drawn sleigh. As this was to be my last social outing for many years its impressions remain clearly. The company was wonderful, the food good and drink excellent, and we danced the night away to a gypsy orchestra and a dance band.

Occasionally through that winter, Kurt would babysit to let me escape for a few hours from our small room. I often went to a nearby coffee house where I could enjoy balalaika music, read German-language newspapers and feast on a plate of Viennese sausages with potato salad. The meals were always very good value for money.

By the spring of 1939 I was fed up with our grumpy landlady and the space constraints of our room. I went apartment-hunting in the countryside and knew of available ones because they were marked with paper crosses on the windows. We found a tiny apartment in a *datcha* which had a beautiful garden. As we had very few possessions we could move house very quickly and I recall that over our two and a half years in Estonia we moved house six times. Our new accommodation was, in reality, only a flatlet on the first floor. It comprised a sparsely furnished room and a kitchen. A very pleasant Estonian family lived on the ground floor and, as the mother looked so young, I remember that, for a long time, I thought she was the sister of the teenage boys. We also had a friend within walking distance whom we could visit. The biggest asset was the garden where I could leave Ruth in her playpen. I had one major scare when she managed to undo the playpen clip and escaped on all fours on to the road. Luckily I got to her in time and picked her up unharmed.

After experiencing the arctic cold of the winter and the long cool spring, it was a treat at last to enjoy the warm summer. The daylight stretched far into the warm nights, which never became dark because we were so far north.

Surviving the Nazis, Exile and Siberia

There were lots of berries to be picked in the woods and a local swimming pool which we visited a few times. It was at this swimming pool that Ruth took her first steps.

During that summer I fell ill with chickenpox. Ruth was about 14 months at the time and the doctor advised that there was no point in separating the child from me. Ruth, luckily, did not contract the disease. This convinced me that breast-feeding, in our case for ten months, immunises a baby. We had to engage a nurse to look after me and the child. In due course the disease abated and the nurse sent me to a bathhouse and instructed me to scrub my skin until all traces of the rash had gone. It was my first visit to a Russian bathhouse. In one part of the bathhouse there were benches and wooden buckets that you filled with hot water which you poured over yourself after scrubbing. In the other was a steamhouse which was very popular with the Estonians and the Russians.

In July 1939 our request to go to Australia was approved and our entry permit arrived. We hoped to leave soon for Australia and our plan was to be united with my parents there. Father had packed and sent all my parent's furniture to storage in Italy to await further instructions for shipment to Australia. Our hopes were high.

Our optimism was soon shattered, however. War broke out at the beginning of September and, as German nationals, our permits became automatically invalid. We were faced with an indefinite stay in Estonia.

In the autumn we moved back into the city to a room in a house that backed on to the radio factory where Kurt worked. He had only to climb over the fence to get to work. Another advantage was that, as we had agreed full board with the landlady, I did not have to cook. I was extremely glad of this as I was pregnant again and happy to take it easy.

By now we had many friends in Tallinn. They would often call after work for a chat, knowing we would always be at

Estonia: September 1938–June 1941

home. This became our main form of entertainment through the winter and, as hosts, we always provided sweets and cigarettes. In those days most of the men were heavy smokers and had no idea of the health hazards. Everyone lived very modestly but at times of celebration seemed to go to extremes. I remember particularly going to a birthday party given by our landlady. The table was laden with all sorts of fish dishes, cold meats and salads. As always the vodka was flowing and everyone ended up very inebriated.

With a second child due, we knew there would not be enough room in the present accommodation, and given our resources it was clear that we would have to move out to the country again to obtain an apartment with enough space. So, in March, I went apartment-hunting once more in the country. The baby was due in four weeks and I was determined to be well settled in before its arrival. I had to take the train from Tallinn to the country, where almost everything remained as nature had made it. The particularly long winter had left the village streets and country roads a sticky morass created by the melting snow.

The only way to carry out the search was to trudge from house to house. This was extremely tiring as I was eight months pregnant and, because of the conditions, had to wear heavy lined boots. I was on the point of giving up when I noticed, amongst a group of trees, a house with paper crosses on some upstairs windows. My hopes rose and I was elated when the landlady showed me a lovely ground floor apartment of two rooms and a kitchen. It was exactly what we needed. We moved in two weeks later and commenced the bout of cleaning and scrubbing to get everything ready for the new baby.

Some days after we had settled, I began to realise that I was going to give birth fairly soon. I got Kurt to organise our trip to Tallinn and went directly to the Itskovits who had offered to take care of Ruth whilst I was in hospital. They lived about five minutes walk from the hospital. I almost left things too late as my son Walter was born within an hour of my admission. All went well and, as soon as he was born, a very strong male nurse lifted me from my bed in the labour ward and carried me to a bed in a general ward. As they were constantly under pressure for beds, I had to leave hospital after five days. We returned to the Itskovits' apartment and remained there until the circumcision, which had to be performed on the eighth day after birth.

I was delighted to get back to our apartment in the country. That spring became one of the happiest times of my life. I loved our accommodation, the area was beautiful and peaceful and I concentrated on looking after my two lovely children. For Ruth's second birthday on 4 May, Mrs Itskovits sprang a delightful surprise. She brought a number of her friends out from the city for a party. They arrived laden with cake, sandwiches, cups and plates and, of course, birthday presents. I look back now and see her as one of the most generous and thoughtful people I have ever known. We were all blissfully happy on that warm spring day.

Our happiness was not to last. It was abruptly cut short in June 1940. Russian planes appeared in the sky to back up the Soviet army which rolled in from the east into Lithuania on the 17 June. Within a month the Baltic States had lost their freedom and independence. Suddenly we found ourselves inside the Soviet Union. It was all so reminiscent of Vienna in 1938, especially when the three states voted in July to become part of the USSR. I cried and became increasingly apprehensive about our future, and if, indeed, we had any future at all. All our neighbours tried to console me: 'Don't worry. The Russians are human. It will be all right', they kept saying. However, I was convinced a new chapter in my life was about to begin.

As the non-aggression pact between Hitler and Stalin was

Estonia: September 1938–June 1941

then still in force we were not regarded as enemy aliens and so we could live and work as before. However, all our friends in business felt the changes at once. All factories and businesses were taken over by the state. The owner of the radio factory where Kurt was employed voluntarily handed over his firm to his workers. He was popular and was retained as an ordinary employee. I thought him a lovely person as I had got to know him quite well. I had given him English lessons in exchange for Russian ones.

The living space for each person was decreed at nine square metres. If the police discovered any excess space they moved lodgers into the building. Our dear friends, the Itskovits, lost their business, their house and their apartment and were forced to live in one room. Mrs Itskovits found a job as a seamstress, but her husband could not find any work. This was an enormous change to their way of life.

Summer and early autumn of 1940 was a sad period in my life. We got news that my grandmother Anna, father's mother, had died in Vienna and then, in September, we were told that my dear father had died in a hospital in Vienna. He was only fifty-nine. His tuberculosis became chronic as a result of the awful conditions imposed on Jews in Vienna in the last two years of his life. When mother moved to England in early 1939, father went to live with his mother. Grandmother was then eighty-five and needed constant help and companionship. Father never, ever, complained in his letters to us but we knew that, as a Jew, he was going through hell under the Nazis. I'm sure he gave his mother most of whatever nourishing food was available and didn't take enough care of himself. After Walter's birth in Tallinn he asked several times for photographs of his two grandchildren. I took some photographs but never sent them because I thought they were not good enough. Now it was too late and I felt very guilty. This prompted me to go to a professional

Surviving the Nazis, Exile and Siberia

photographer and to send copies to my mother in London. This was to be our last communication with my mother until the war was over. Looking back at those times from a distance I feel that perhaps father was lucky that he died when he did, as some months later the transportations from Vienna to the death camps were under way.

In the autumn of 1940 the apartment of a friend in Tallinn became vacant and we were offered the tenancy. It was part of a traditional-style Estonian house. The apartment had a cellar and a loft and at 36 square metres was the correct size for the four of us. The previous tenant had been able to raise three children there. We accepted the tenancy gladly, especially because we would not be forced to accept lodgers. It turned out to be a very cosy apartment. The tiled stove gave good heat in the hall and the two bedrooms. The kitchen stove heated a tiled wall in our living room. We knew this would be essential for the winter ahead.

As soon as the Russian occupation forces arrived their wives proceeded to buy up all the Western textiles, clothes and footwear in the shops. They knew that no new supplies would come into the country and so the shelves were emptied within days. This, of course, was hastened by the Soviet authorities who had told all the Russian immigrants that the shops were laden with merchandise because the Estonians were too poor to buy it. The Soviet occupation forces were well paid and could afford to do this. Soon the Estonians grew relatively poorer as their pay remained fixed while the price of food and everything else rose steeply. This created a divided society and much resentment on the part of the indigenous population.

We lived near the central markets which allowed me to shop frequently and stockpile as much as possible. As food got dearer and scarcer by the day I built up stocks of cocoa, chocolate, sugar, noodles, soap and much else. I dried mushrooms, made a lot of jam and rendered butter, which I

Estonia: September 1938–June 1941

stored in the cellar. I was always apprehensive about whether this would see us through the long winter.

I tried to make life as interesting and busy as possible. Apart from my involvement with the children my two main interests were reading and developing a small button-making business. There were many books in Estonian libraries in German and so I could borrow a range of titles. Two particular books that I borrowed were to influence me in the immediate years ahead. The first gave me a great insight into life in Siberia, particularly into camp life. It described the flight of a White Russian officer from the communists. He had a number of encounters with Kasakhs and other tribesmen, and endured many hardships crossing the Taiga to reach India, his ultimate goal. The second book was Dostoevsky's *From a Dead House*, now also an opera, which describes life in the Siberian camp to which he had been exiled. Our experiences in the years ahead confirmed that conditions hadn't changed much in a century. Little did I know how relevant these books were to be.

I was offered the use of a button-making machine which I saw as an opportunity to earn some extra money. Soon I was so busy producing buttons for dressmakers that I had to engage a daily home-help. As I had a working knowledge of the Estonian language, I could do the daily round of my customers on foot and take orders, make deliveries and sort out any problems. In the evenings, Kurt and I made the cloth-covered buttons. Luckily, I had taken out a manufacturing licence. Someone denounced me to the police for working illegally, but when they made their inspection, the police found everything in order.

The greatest advantage in living without a lodger was that we could listen in secret, with close friends, to the BBC. This was totally illegal and, if caught, would have incurred a severe penalty. As a neighbour was an Estonian officer we had to keep the sound to a minimum and restricted our listening to news only. It was the only accurate source of information on the war and the world outside; no one could believe what they read in the local newspapers. During that winter and the spring of 1941 we grew more apprehensive as we tracked the progress of the war. We wondered about Lotte and mother's fate during September's Battle of Britain. We had no way of knowing whether they had survived the terrible pounding of London. More ominous was the imprisonment of the Warsaw Jews into the ghetto in November. All through early 1941 we heard of German success in pushing across Eastern Europe and of further London air raids. As always, we feared that Jews would suffer in these territories. This was confirmed by news of many restrictions on the rights of French Jews from May.

On the morning of 15 June I was surprised by a strange event in the yard at the back of the apartment. The people from the house opposite were being rounded up and herded into a lorry parked in the yard. Shortly after, the guards got back on to the lorry which drove quickly away. I had no sense of foreboding; I was merely puzzled. What crime had the whole family committed? Then Kurt returned unexpectedly from work at 10 a.m. He brought the shattering news that all the so-called 'bourgeoisie' were being rounded up and transported to Siberian camps. His former boss was amongst them. The event earlier now made sense to me. The people opposite were arrested because they used to own a shoe shop.

I immediately thought of our great friends, the Itskovits, who had done so much for us and other immigrant Jews. I rushed to their apartment house but I was already too late to see them. They had been arrested during the night. I next sought out their daughter, Berta, who had a room not far from us. She told me that her parents had been taken to Tallinn harbour to await transportation. We decided to go there together. At the harbour there was a large and noisy crowd

Estonia: September 1938–June 1941

trying to break through the cordon of soldiers to reach the trains containing the prisoners. Eventually we succeeded in getting through and then came face-to-face with a scene which really shocked both of us. The prisoners were all locked up in cattle trucks. Women and children were staring through the grills of the small windows. On another track were the trucks with the men, also locked up. After a long search we found Mrs Itskovits. We managed to give her some money, photographs and a watch. Apart from saying a tearful goodbye, that was all we could do. I was glad I had seen her but greatly disturbed that she would shortly be on the horrific journey to Siberia with all those other unfortunate people.

When I came home and described to Kurt what I had witnessed, we decided that we should be prepared for the worst. We suspected that foreigners like ourselves were likely to be next to be sent into exile. We bought suitcases and leather strappings. The following night we heard many heavy footsteps on the wooden stairs. My heart pounded wildly and I said to Kurt, 'This is it!' I was certain it was our turn. However, no one knocked on our door. Next morning we learnt that our neighbour, the Estonian army officer, had been arrested.

Shortly everything was to change for ever. On 22 June Hitler broke the non-aggression pact and attacked the Soviet Union. We were now converted into enemy aliens. Soon after, when we were listening to BBC news with friends, another friend came to collect her sister. The NKVD (the secret police) were at their apartment to arrest them.

10 · Harju Camp, Estonia: July 1941

We did not have long to wait for the knock on our door. A high-ranking Soviet officer and two soldiers had arrived to arrest us. Because we could not understand Russian, a neighbour was instructed by them to act as interpreter. Their message was abrupt and succinct: 'Pack what you'll need for a year away from here!'

We took a long time to pack because we had planned to take as much as possible. We filled our suitcases and then made up bundles. We packed summer and winter clothing, bedding including mattresses, cooking utensils, bowls and buckets, the indispensable primus cooker, the baby's pushchair and most of our hoarded provisions. When our home-help heard of the arrests of enemy aliens, she calmly said to me: 'When you're arrested, I'll take the bed of the master and the standard lamp!' In the end she got nothing because the secret police locked up the apartment. We got no opportunity either to settle her outstanding wages.

When the officer counted our 17 cases and bundles he sent for a lorry. Whilst we waited, the first ever air-raid alarm sounded. We all went down into the cellar and sat in the dark until the all-clear was given. At the time we did not realise how lucky we were to be able to take so much with us. Later, we discovered that, as the war heightened, people could only take what they could carry. Many, too, were arrested on the streets and transported without any belongings.

Harju Camp, Estonia: July 1941

Finally, when the lorry was loaded, the four of us had to sit atop all our worldly goods. Kurt held Ruth and I nursed Walter; Ruth was then three and Walter was 14 months. It was a bright summer morning. Kurt and I were not depressed but rather excited at the beginning of an unknown adventure. We were driven to Harju Detention Camp about 20 miles east of Tallinn. The camp was in a row of barracks attached to a large prison. In the detention camp were about 150 enemy aliens rounded up from all over Estonia. Included were many nationalities – Austrian, Czech, German, Slovak and, of course, *Balten-Deutsche*. Almost half of the total were recent Jewish refugees from Austria and Germany.

Women and children were locked up separately at night from the men. I remember the first time when it really struck me that I was now a prisoner. I was refused permission to go to the toilet and was made to wait until several women were to go together. We were escorted by camp staff. Apart from the separation at night, the regime was relatively lax. We were all allowed to mix during the day and they decided to give us access to the prison bathhouse. In general, the camaraderie was very good in the first few days and a few people there became life-long friends. Eggs and milk were on sale. I worried so much that my children would suffer from malnutrition that I fed them too many eggs. Walter, not used to eggs, broke out all over in a rash, causing me to alter his diet at once.

The Nazi advance eastward was so rapid that it was necessary, after only ten days at Harju, to move us by train further eastwards into Russia. As a special concession, because of the young children, I did not have to walk to the train like all the other prisoners. The three of us were given a lift in a Black Maria. It was a very gruesome experience, being shaken about in the dark, because of the blacked-out windows and not knowing where we were going or how long the journey would take.

When we arrived at the railway point, a cattle train was waiting. There were no steps or ladders on to the high trucks. Unless you were very athletic and young you required a helping hand to board the train. Each truck had two-tiered bunks at each end, small windows with grills and a hole in the floor, which served as a toilet. The toilet arrangement was particularly dehumanising and embarrassing because, on this journey, men and women travelled together, with 25 of us packed into each truck. The six trucks required a seventh to hold our luggage and kitchen facilities.

I can still recollect the almost unbearable humidity and discomfort travelling in the July heat. The children grew very restless and I had to take Walter's clothes off and sponge him down. Suddenly, and without warning, we heard the German planes coming from the south-west. We were eastbound on the line running almost parallel with the southern shore of the Gulf of Finland and approaching the town of Narva, on the old Soviet border with Estonia. The train contained a series of fuel tanks and was an obvious target.

We stopped abruptly. We then saw all our accompanying soldiers scurry into the nearby woods. They were well aware of the fatal explosions should the fuel tanks get bombed. We were left fully exposed on the line and locked into our trucks. It was then we realised how dispensable we had all become. Shortly after the bombing started, a bomb scored a direct hit on one of the trucks and blew the door off the adjoining one. Luckily the fuel tanks escaped.

Shortly after the explosion someone unlocked the door of our truck. We scrambled out and ran into the woods to hide. Walter started howling because his naked body was attacked by a horde of midges. One woman saved the day. She lent me a sheet to protect him and he quietened down.

Harju Camp, Estonia: July 1941

We could see that one of the bombers had circled back to have a second look. The pilot must have been satisfied with the destruction or perhaps all the bombs had been used. The plane kept going westwards. Sadly ten people died and 11 were injured in the truck which suffered the direct hit. Amongst the dead was a mother whose son and husband escaped unhurt. Amongst the injured, who had to be left behind in Narva, were an eminent cancer specialist from Berlin and his two daughters. A mother and daughter ran away as, presumably, like most of the German population in Estonia, they welcomed the invading Nazis as salvation from the Soviet occupation.

When all went quiet the Soviet soldiers returned and herded us back on to the train. We then began our 800-mile journey which ended four days later in Gorki (Nishny Novgorod). The heat and humidity was made a little more bearable because we were now allowed to leave the truck door open. It was impossible and futile to try to escape, because each truck was heavily guarded and, if we did get away from the train, we would have had a very brief freedom in Soviet territory. Our diet consisted of 'dry rations' as no cooking was done on the train. These included bread, salted fish, biscuits and a little tea substitute. This diet exacerbated our thirst in the heat because of the high salt content in the fish and the lack of enough tea substitute. We didn't dare drink unboiled water. Now that our door was open we could look out – and people looked in. At times we stopped alongside trains taking Russian evacuees eastwards. When they saw our children they spontaneously handed over chocolates and other 'goodies'. I also remember seeing a train with convicts who were treated very roughly and other trains which were so crowded that some people were sitting on carriage bumpers and roofs. Once, one of our companions had the temerity to sing a very popular song which translated means: 'I do not know of any country where man breathes as freely as here'. One of the soldiers heard it and, furious, slammed the door of our truck shut as a punishment.

Tension built up throughout the journey because we never knew where we were, where we were going or when our frequent stops would be over. The journey was a series of delays and movements. We assumed that the railways were giving priority to Soviet army movement of troops and equipment because we were generally relegated to night travel with interminable stops in between. We had travelled south-east, skirted Moscow and then went eastwards for about 300 miles to Gorki. At first we thought it was just another stopover, but, as soon as the train stopped there, we were ordered to disembark.

11 · Oranki Camp, Gorki: July–November 1941

As soon as we disembarked and assembled our belongings we were taken to a local monastery at Oranki which had been converted into a prison camp. The monastery chapel was used as a storeroom and the refectory had been transformed into a male dormitory, with three-tiered wooden bunks. Women and children were housed in smaller buildings.

My first impression was of a holiday camp. There were lots of young children running around wearing bathing trunks. Two friendly young women served us refreshing cold tea. Next we were taken to the bathhouse and disinfection room. After being unable to wash for over four days, this was most welcome. We were led to a changing room and ordered to take all our clothes off and then thread them on to a wire hoop which transported them into a heat chamber for disinfection. Next we filed into the washroom which had rows of benches with wooden tubs. We all had to queue to get hot water from the old man who ladled it from a cauldron into the tubs. He seemed oblivious to our nakedness. First I scrubbed down Ruth and Walter and then washed myself. Then I had to wash my hair with the yellow paste we had been given. All went well until inadvertently I got some suds in my eyes. They smarted so acutely that I thought I had been blinded. I didn't know that the yellow paste was some sulphuric concoction for killing headlice. Copious use of cold water eased the pain gradually. We went from the washroom to the dressing room where our disinfected clothes awaited us. One woman went into hysterics when she discovered that her only dress had fallen into the heat chamber fire and was completely destroyed. She had to make do with a horrible hand-out from the camp store.

When we arrived there were already a lot of people interned there as enemy aliens. They had been rounded up in other places throughout the Soviet Union and beyond – from Riga, Moscow, the Black Sea and the Danube. Some had been arrested at sea or on the river. There was no compulsory work, but many volunteered to carry out duties because this entitled them to extra bread and other food. A number volunteered to staff the kitchen and the bathhouse as well as other services. Kurt applied to be given the ingredients for the food rations allowed for our family and asked for a place in the kitchen. He was issued with vegetables, cooking oil, potatoes and a little bit of meat. He supplemented these with some of the provisions we had brought from home in Estonia and cooked all our meals in the communal kitchen. The arrival of a new commandant abruptly ended this cosy arrangement.

The new commandant brought in a stricter regime. He introduced daily head counts in the yard. This was an uncomfortable nuisance whilst we stood for lengthy periods in the summer heat. However, when the weather became very cold and wintry later in the year, the count turned into a real hardship. We all stood there until everyone was accounted for. It usually took over an hour and we would have to stand there unprotected in rain or frost or snow.

One day an order to shave the heads of all the children was issued. This was carried out as a precaution against the possible spread of typhus. Both Ruth and Walter had lovely long blonde curls then, as their hair had never been cut before. It was a shock to see them with shaven heads. I remember thinking that they looked rather like tadpoles!

Oranki Camp, Gorki: July–November 1941

In November the order came to pack all our belongings and get prepared for another transfer east because the German army was penetrating even deeper into the Soviet Union. By then they were outside Moscow, Leningrad, Kharkov and in the Crimea. They were also progressing towards Solechnaya Gora, 40 miles north-west of Moscow. The Soviet government had moved to Kuybyshev, 500 miles east of Moscow.

We were marched to the railway point and there stood the now familiar cattle-truck carriages. This train contained about 15 trucks to cater for 300 internees. This time we found a little iron stove in the middle of the truck. It was not very effective because our clothes still froze to the sides of the truck overnight. We were quite well fed on the journey and thought our two dishes of hot gruel daily was really quite exceptional. With the stove we were able to brew tea substitute to which I would add a shot of cognac. (Since leaving home I had concealed the cognac in the nappy bundle and got it clear through each search.) I shared my doctored tea with a French lady who was one of the people who occupied the bunk next to us. The bunks were made from bare wooden planks, put together. On this journey the men were segregated from the women and children.

My French companion was called Jeanne Saunier. She had seven-year-old twins, Sylvia and Jeannot. All three helped me to practise my French and we became very close friends. After her husband had been exiled to Siberia for having studied and lived abroad, Jeanne became a governess at the French embassy in Moscow. It was only after the war that she discovered that her husband was living in the very town that we were now going to, and at the same time.

The journey proceeded with the usual stops and starts, the reasons for which were never explained. The Russian trains had a terrifying way of stopping and starting which jolted the trucks backwards and forwards violently with a noisy clatter. I had to keep protecting the children from injury and so I placed myself across their feet to prevent them being knocked off the top bunk, which we shared with six others.

The journey seemed interminable. We travelled through endless lowland areas and mountains alternately. The countryside had a continual bleakness as everywhere was covered in snow. In central Russia at that time of year night temperatures sink to as low as −20°C.

We travelled south from Gorki to Penza and stopped outside the city for some time. As always, our journey restarted unexpectedly. We then went east to Kuybyshev, crossing the Volga at Syzran, and had another long stop. Then we progressed south-east to the city of Chkalov (Orenburg) where we were delayed for some time. Each time we stopped I left the train and went to fetch water. I felt that this was my duty because I was the biggest user of water, due to the needs of my two children. At Chkalov the weather was so cold that my bucket froze to the well. Luckily, the soldier escort was able to release it and I arrived back with my full quota of water.

All through the journey wild rumours spread. One was that all the men would be sent to a separate camp. Another was that all the Jews would be sent to Birobidzhan, the so-called Jewish autonomous region in the Far East. We didn't know before then that this area existed. The rumour persisted and we were told that the climate there was horrific. Throughout the journey we were thus apprehensive about our eventual fate. We left Chkalov and headed further south, crossing into Kazakhstan. Eventually, after a total journey of over five days from Gorki – a distance of 800 miles – we arrived at our destination outside the Kazakh city of Aktyubinsk.

12 · Aktyubinsk Camp, Kazakhstan: November 1941–July 1942

When the truck doors opened we saw that we had stopped in the middle of a snow-covered field. We were shown in which direction to walk. Carrying Walter in one arm and keeping a tight grip on Ruth's hand with the other, I made very slow progress plodding through the deep snow. After some time, I glimpsed the outlines of a watchtower in the distance. I knew then I had gone in the right direction.

At last, when we reached the gate of the camp, a guard led us to a large hut. Of course, everyone else was already there as they had reached the hut long before me and the children. The floor was covered with exhausted bodies. I had difficulty finding a space for myself and the children. The situation was chaotic and very distressing. It had not been caused by any cruelty or malicious intent; rather it was due to lack of communication. The camp commandant had received orders to prepare for 300 new arrivals. He had assumed they would all be men. He panicked when he saw the women and children. Determined to keep the sexes apart, he divided the camp with a hastily erected barbed wire fence and sent the men to their prepared barracks, with their two-tiered bunks. The women and children were forced to remain in the large unfurnished hut for two days until barracks were fixed up to accommodate us.

Amidst all this confusion I saw a face from the past. We

both recognised each other at once and hugged joyously. It was Herta Schwarz, a Viennese actress and singer who had played in many musicals. She and her husband, a composer and pianist, were guests in 1932 at the boarding house where I had my first job. I was overjoyed to meet someone from my past and with whom I could share memories of Vienna. They had fled, with their little daughter, to Riga in 1939 and had been arrested there in July.

Herta and I decided that we would stick together. When eventually we were directed to bunks we settled down side by side. Again the bunks were simply bare wooden planks. They were fitted in on either end and a second tier above. I remember clearly, on a night when I couldn't sleep, counting how many people I could reach without moving from my bunk. I thought it would not be believed if I were to recount it someday, if we were ever to get out. I could reach 11 people. There were three to my left, three to my right and five on the bunk backing on to our line.

Each bunk measured about 3ft by 6ft, with the two children sharing one. All our possessions had to be kept under the palliasse on which we slept or on the floor under the bunks. Because I had two small children I had to have a bucket of water, a bowl and a potty nearby at all times. Keeping the little ones amused and clean became a constant nightmare. All I could do was have them sit there all day because their clothes and footwear were totally inadequate for the arctic cold outside. The winter temperatures there could fall to about −20°C during the day and to about −30°C at night. As there was no room for them to play or walk indoors, they were virtually immobile all the time. Every day constant effort was required to keep them occupied.

Conditions were primitive and the whole experience dreadful. This, of course, was exacerbated by the severity of the winter conditions in Kazakhstan, with deep snow and

1. *Edith with her mother and Lotte, 1918.*

2. Mother, father, Kurt and Edith, Vienna, 1934.

3. *The aircraft that brought Edith and family to Tallinn, 1938.*

4. *Edith with Ruth, two, and baby Walter, Estonia, 1940.*

5. *Official photograph of Edith with Leah, two, Walter, seven, Ruth, nine, and Kurt, Vienna 1947.*

6. From left to right: Leah, Edith, Ruth, Kurt with Esther, and Walter, Kilkeel, 1954.

7. Brian Faulkener, Northern Ireland Minister of Commerce, visits the Company's stand in Gothenburg, Sweden, 1968.

8. Edith and Kurt celebrate their golden wedding, 1986.

9. Golden wedding present; a photograph of the family with staff at the foot of the Mourne Mountains, 1986.

10. Peak of achievement; a small selection of customer labels.

11. Edith introduces Walter to The Princess Royal at the Men's International Fashion Fair, Paris, 1989.

12. Enjoying their retirement; Edith and Kurt on holiday in the Bahamas, 1996.

Aktyubinsk Camp, Kazakhstan: November 1941–July 1942

freezing conditions day and night. Our large hut was heated by a single stove in one corner and was lit by a single kerosene lamp. This meant that we spent the whole winter shivering in semi-darkness. As washing and toilet facilities were out in the open yard, we had to face the arctic conditions frequently. There were crude basins in the open yard where we could wash our faces and hands and once a month we were taken to a bathhouse. My nights were usually disturbed by the need to visit the toilet. This required getting fully dressed and then finding my way in the dark across the yard to get to the toilet hut. I developed great stealth as I hardly ever roused the children from their sleep. It then took at least an hour to warm up again and get to sleep.

The food in the camp was awful. Our diet consisted of watery soups, a tasteless gruel made from oats or millet and a chunk of bread. Occasionally we would get a piece of salted fish. Each person had been issued with a wooden dish and wooden spoon. These were brightly decorated and we were told this was traditional art made by monks. Nowadays similar dishes can be bought in souvenir shops in Russia. Fortunately, we still had the cutlery we had brought out of Vienna. I have always maintained that the best food can be ruined by eating it with a wooden spoon, whereas tasteless food can be made almost tolerable if eaten with a silver spoon.

We used to have great enjoyment by forming language groups. We had a small group for English conversation and had one person who taught Spanish. I practised French often, as I always spoke it in conversation with my friend Jeanne Saunier. Once a week a *Politruk* (political instructor) would arrive and read out the latest news from the newspaper. We then would discuss this in various languages. Most of the news was from the war front and in the winter of 1941–42 was extremely distressing. Week after week, we heard of the German advances eastwards. We did not doubt the news that was read to us but, looking back now, I cannot decide whether much of what the *Politruk* told us was propaganda or the truth.

There was one amazing incident that winter which I knew I would never forget. It taught me how resilient people can be when all the odds are against them.

The incident concerned a mother and her child, Erika. While we were in the Gorki camp a Romanian family called Nacht arrived there. The family consisted of the parents and two sons. Whilst there, they refused to mix with other inmates and spoke only Romanian amongst themselves. They were transported to the Aktyubinsk Camp in our train and Mrs Nacht ended up in our hut. She became totally depressed very quickly. She completely neglected herself and refused to change her clothes, to wash or to clean her hair. As she became full of lice she became a danger to the rest of us in the barrack. Eventually, we discovered she was expecting a baby.

Some years later, when we ended up sharing a room, she told me what had happened to her. When she arrived at Aktyubinsk she asked the camp doctor for a termination to her pregnancy. Her application was sent off and the reply took weeks. Then she was taken into the town's hospital where the doctor refused to operate because her pregnancy was too advanced. At that point, deep depression set in. The thought of having to bring up a baby in camp conditions terrified her. But nature took its course.

In January, Mrs Nacht asked the visiting lady doctor to send her to the hospital for confinement. The doctor refused, maintaining that children weren't born as quickly as that. The following night Mrs Nacht went into labour in the barrack. Our own nurse, a fellow internee who worked as a professional nurse in the camp dispensary, asked her, 'Do you want to give birth here or drive to the hospital?' Of course, she elected to be driven to hospital rather than go through this very personal event in front of all the women and children in the hut.

Aktyubinsk Camp, Kazakhstan: November 1941–July 1942

It took some time before a horse and sleigh were made ready. Mrs Nacht was covered with lots of blankets to protect her on the long journey in the freezing winter night. The nurse went with her. They chatted for a while until Mrs Nacht went very quiet. After some time she said to the nurse, 'The baby is born.' They were both worried that the baby might be suffocated under all the blankets but they couldn't expose it to the arctic conditions. Luckily, the baby survived. When they reached the hospital they had difficulty getting admitted because the baby was already born. However, our nurse took no nonsense and insisted that they be admitted. The nurse then had to go back to the camp. After a few days Mrs Nacht returned to the camp with her new baby. She was named Erika and became the star of our barracks. From then on, Mrs Nacht's depression lifted, and by the time I parted from her, Erika was a strapping four-year-old.

In spite of the cramped conditions and the miserable food and climate, Ruth and Walter seemed to develop satisfactorily. Then, suddenly one day, Walter developed a high fever and a rash. He was 20 months old. The visiting doctor suspected scarlet fever and ordered him to be taken to the isolation hospital. I dressed him in his warmest clothes and wrapped him in many blankets to protect him on the long journey in an open sleigh. The hospital confirmed scarlet fever. Very reluctantly I left him as I was not allowed to stay and had to return to the camp. Once in a while a soldier would come up to me and say, 'I have seen your little boy in hospital. He is all right. I gave him a biscuit'. I was always glad to hear this although I could never bring myself fully to believe him.

Weeks passed without news from the hospital. I was getting more worried by the day. When I thought it was time for the fever to have passed and for Walter's release from hospital I went to the camp commandant to find out about the delay. He replied, 'I can't get the child back because all his clothes have been burned in the disinfection chamber'. I suspected that it was more likely that someone had taken a fancy to the good quality Western clothes. I put another outfit together, gave it to the commandant and begged him to have the child brought back.

Two days later a nurse arrived with Walter. We hardly recognised him. His head was swathed in bandages. He was as light as a new-born baby. He could not sit or stand. Kurt was so upset when he saw his son that he cried. (It was the only time in the years of our ordeals that I saw him cry.) Walter had undergone an operation on his glands and had contracted chickenpox as well as scarlet fever. He had eaten very little throughout his stay in hospital. He must have felt very unhappy and lost in hospital, because everyone spoke Russian, which he did not understand.

I suspect that I got him back just in time. Some people predicted cruelly that he was bound to die anyway. Every night, when I tried to get to sleep, Walter started to yell. He calmed down only when I walked him up and down from wall to wall. One day a woman complained to the commandant about this nightly disturbance. I was called to his office to be asked, 'What is wrong with your child? Why does he cry so much?'. I replied that the child cried from hunger because there was no food suitable to feed him with. The commandant then took me to the storeroom and gave me a kilo of noodles and a kilo of semolina. Abruptly he told me, 'Here, feed your child properly.'

These rations helped Walter quite a bit but he remained very slow regaining his strength. One day, when I took him to the first aid station, a Polish medical orderly said to me, 'We could try something that would really help your child. If you agree, we could try blood transfusions.' He suggested drawing blood from a vein in my arm and injecting the blood into Walter's buttock. He did that ten times at two-day intervals and it worked wonders! Gradually the child gained

Aktyubinsk Camp, Kazakhstan: November 1941–July 1942

weight but it was to take a full year before he was back to the normal development for his age.

Winter came to a fairly abrupt end towards the end of April. The spring sun was now so strong that it created steam as it melted the deep layer of snow in the yard. There was a danger that all the barracks would be flooded. As a precaution we were moved quickly to a building on higher ground at the back of the camp. Unfortunately, the building hadn't any bunks and so we slept on the floor. There was no bathhouse or toilets. We had to use the back of the building for toilet facilities and, as far as possible, stood guard for each other to create some modicum of privacy.

After about a week we were moved back to our original huts as the snow had all disappeared. Unexpectedly, some days later, all the able-bodied men were rounded up and sent off to a local brick factory to work. This was the first time Kurt and I were separated.

During the early months of 1942 the weekly session given by the *Politruk* brought news of fluctuating fortunes. We had heard of the Germans being routed at Moscow in December and then of the German advances on the Kerch Peninsula in the Crimea. We were proudly told of the successes of the Red Army in May when it pierced the German 'hedgehog' positions at Kharkov. Bad news followed as we were told of the advance of the Germans towards the Don and the Volga. The *Politruk* told us that their key objective seemed to be Stalingrad. We felt somewhat apprehensive because we knew there was little resistance eastwards from that city. All that was between us and the Volga was 500 miles of open plain.

Work kept our minds off our worries about survival and the possible consequences of German victory. Work brigades were recruited to work on the farms outside. We found this work a form of escape from the camp which had become very claustrophobic in the hot summer weather, when the place was permeated by the obnoxious smell from the latrines. My actress friend Herta and I decided to volunteer for work on alternate days and to look after our children on the other days. Apart from escaping the confined space of the camp our work earned a double supper and double portion of bread each evening on our return from the fields.

We were driven to and from the work sites in open lorries. My very first work detail was in a team of 20 women told to weed a field of carrots. As I had never before seen how anything grew in a field, I had no idea of how to distinguish the carrot seedlings from the weeds I was supposed to attack with the hoe. I imagine there were no carrots left on the patch I weeded. It was exhilarating to get out and move in the warm open air. The field was so vast you couldn't see the edges of it in any direction. We brewed tea and baked potatoes on an open fire and, all the time, fraternised with the guards. We knew that we could gain some freedoms and that the guards wouldn't upset the situation. This duty roster was more like a holiday for all these young soldiers.

Another work detail teamed me with a Yugoslav boatman, who had been arrested as an enemy alien on a ship in the Danube. We were told to plough a field in preparation for planting potatoes. I was to lead the horse and he was to guide the plough. As I had never been near a horse in my life, I was scared it might kick me or snap at me. He showed me how to treat the animal and off we went, breaking the soil in fairly straight furrows. As the day was very hot, I took off my shoes. It was a most satisfying sensation to feel the warm earth under my feet. We kept working in the field for a number of days until we had sown the seed potatoes and covered the drills. I also learnt to plant cabbages. Little did I appreciate then how my agricultural experiences would come in very useful in later life.

During that summer I felt very fit and strong. Some days

Aktyubinsk Camp, Kazakhstan: November 1941–July 1942

in the fields I volunteered to fetch two buckets of water with which to make our lunch. The river was about half a mile away, down a steep embankment. My secret plan was to have a dip in the cool water. It was a delicious luxury which no one ever suspected I had snatched on my journey to the river.

One day, the guard at work was the same soldier who had brought me messages during the winter about Walter's progress in the hospital. We had a long chat. He was very worried and very sad, and glad to have someone to talk to. He told me that it was his last day of duty in our camp before being sent to the front. He was allowed two days to say goodbye to his mother and his daughter who lived together. His attitude convinced me then that his messages about Walter had, in fact, been the truth. I felt sorry for him because he was leaving for the front at the most intense period of the war so far, and his chances of survival were probably quite poor.

In July, at the height of summer, the order came to pack everything and prepare for another transportation. We assumed that the Germans were advancing further east. All the men were brought back to the camp from the brick factory. To my consternation, Kurt was hobbling on crutches. He had a wound on the sole of his foot which had become infected and caused a thrombosis. He was not allowed to step on the ground with the infected foot. Otherwise he looked well and was in good spirits.

When we were all packed and ready to leave, our departure was postponed for 24 hours. It was a balmy summer evening. I did not want to go to sleep yet, especially on the bare boards that were left. In the yard I met up with an engineer from Vienna with whom I had occasionally discussed music and opera. We sat on a bench and whistled the whole of Beethoven's violin concerto in unison. It was an evening of joy I have never forgotten.

Next day we had to walk to the railway point where the train with the customary cattle trucks awaited us. Our journey from the camp to the railway seemed so much shorter than on our arrival in the deep winter snow.

Our journey was more bearable than the one in the arctic conditions of the winter, although we had the usual stops and starts. We went north-east some 250 miles to Kartaly and then through Kustanay to the city of Akmolinsk (now Celinograd), some 600 miles south-east. We passed through railway stations with beautiful flowers and saw many women in cheerful print dresses, mostly red. At each stop I went on my usual search for water. Once, on one of these excursions, a soldier threatened to shoot me if I turned my head around again. I had only looked to see if my companion was following, but he must have had orders to shoot. He couldn't have thought I would try to escape. In another station the train stopped some distance from the well. This involved a very frightening experience because we had to climb over or under stationary trucks to get to the well. We couldn't be sure if the train would suddenly move and crush us. With empty buckets we moved nimbly but the whole thing was nightmarish when we were loaded down with full buckets.

The final part of our four-day journey of about 1,000 miles was the 150 miles through the foothills from Akmolinsk to the city of Karaganda. This was a major centre for coal-mining and industry in Kazakhstan. We were now about 700 miles further east.

13 · *Spaski Camp, Karaganda: July 1942–January 1943*

After our arrival at Karaganda station we were transferred swiftly on to open lorries. We were taken up the mountains to Spaski Camp, a one-hour bumpy ride in the blazing summer sun. After four days' journey in the intense heat we were very weary and glad to rest in our bunks, shortly after arrival at the camp.

Not long after we settled in, I noticed that little Walter was covered in bites. On closer examination we discovered that the bunks were infested with hungry bed bugs. They were paper thin and transparent before they attacked. They would attack small children at any time and seemed to reserve adults for night-time attacks. The situation was so chronic that we asked to sleep out in the open and moved back only after a thorough disinfection.

In Spaski, work started in earnest for every able-bodied internee. As before, the men were rounded up and sent to work in a brick factory. Kurt's foot injury turned out to be a blessing in disguise – he was classified as an invalid and wasn't sent away on work duty. It soon became apparent that the work was too difficult and the diet totally insufficient for a great number of the men. At 2,000 metres, the high altitude exacerbated the problems. Many did not survive and, sadly, they included the husband of Herta, my actress friend.

As in the previous camp, there were work brigades of women sent out to work on the farms. Here there was an added hardship. At the end of each working day, when the workers were often exhausted, each of them had to carry a heavy '*saman*' – a large brick made from sunbaked clay and straw – from the fields into the camp. As I had to look after my children, I did not have to go out to work.

That autumn yielded an outstanding crop of large melons in the area. At first we were delighted to get the fruit. However, our bodies were totally unused to this addition to our diet and soon almost everyone developed chronic diarrhoea. There was a constant queue at the toilets and, when we couldn't wait any longer, we squatted behind our huts. The Russian guards then said we were, *bez culturnye ljudy* – people without any culture. At the time I thought this amusing because I remembered what we had been told in Tallinn in 1940 about the Russian orchestra which had visited the city. Many of them had fouled up backstage because they thought the water closet was for washing in!

The diarrhoea epidemic was very debilitating and work details felt much more onerous and exhausting. That autumn proved a difficult time for everyone. The work got harder, the food was meagre and there was a great lack of medicines. Morale was very low.

These conditions proved to be too much for some. I remember that one young man, whose mother and brother had already died, committed suicide. He had been the brilliant linguist in Tallinn. By then we had an excellent doctor, who had emigrated from Vienna, but there was little he could do to help. The only medicine he had was sodium permanganate, with which he cleaned wounds, gave it as a gargle for throat infections and as a strong solution to cure diarrhoea. At one stage I had to bathe Walter in a weak solution of it to cure sores which appeared all over his body.

Spaski Camp, Karaganda: July 1942–January 1943

Soon after we had settled in, another transport arrived from the West. Among the prisoners were Herta's mother and, luckily, a doctor and a dentist, both from Vienna. This brought the internee population to about 2,000, of some 17 nationalities.

It shortly became evident that women in general and men from poorer countries with simple diets were the most robust and most likely to survive. Men from the Scandinavian countries who had been used to a very rich diet, lost weight and had the lowest resistance. Quite a number of them died fairly quickly.

After a very hot summer and a short autumn, the 1942–43 winter set in abruptly in November with severe frosts and a lot of snow. By then, any news given to us was about the battle of Stalingrad and of the continuing bravery of the Soviet people at the siege of Leningrad. Everyone, including the soldiers, was conscious of the difficulties we would face if Stalingrad fell. We, of course, had no inkling whatsoever of the Holocaust or of the slaughter of Jews in September in Warsaw.

It was then I had to suffer a particularly traumatic ordeal. For some time I had been troubled by one of my wisdom teeth and now the pain had flared up again. The Viennese dentist advised extraction which he carried out in a 20-minute operation without any kind of anaesthetic or painkiller. Although the room was freezing we were both perspiring and completely exhausted at the end.

On a dull winter's day in January the order came to pack up and get ready to march through the snow to the next camp, Kok U Sek, a short distance further up the hill. The rumour was that we had to vacate Spaski to make way for German prisoners of war. I was appalled at the state of the men when I saw them as they lined up in the yard. They had aged tremendously, were haggard and thin and had the grey look of ghosts. When we were all assembled we then trudged through the snow for half an hour to the new site on the hill.

14 · Kok U Sek Camp, Karaganda: January 1943–May 1945

When we got to Kok U Sek we could see Spaski Camp down below us. As we passed through the gates of our new camp I could not see any buildings. They were all fully covered by deep snow. A small passage had been cleared to get us from the camp entrance to the door of our hut.

The camp contained five small huts, completely hidden by snow, where mothers with children were housed and three large barracks with two-tiered bunks for men and women without children. There was a bathhouse/laundry building, a first aid station and a large kitchen dispersed throughout the site of about three acres which was surrounded by two rows of barbed wire with look-out towers at regular intervals.

The small huts were privileged quarters for mothers and children. Each hut had two rooms separated by a big stove. Eleven of us were allocated the larger room and seven the smaller room. We had just enough space for the bunks and small passages between families and about a one-yard passage between the wall and the foot of the bunks. It was incredibly cramped. The two children and I were put into the larger room along with a young German woman, her mother and young son, a Polish woman and her son and an Estonian woman with her two children.

The young German woman was called Lisl Steinbrecher. She was from a wealthy German family who emigrated to

Kok U Sek Camp, Karaganda: January 1943–May 1945

Estonia in the early 1930s and started a button factory there. Unfortunately, Lisl was addicted to certain drugs and kept feigning attacks of kidney pain to obtain them.

The Polish lady, Sidy Menzer, had already spent a year in another Siberian camp, where her husband had died. She said she spent most of that year chopping wood. Her four-year-old son was very lively and kept Sidy occupied a lot of the time. I remember her saying frequently, 'I wish that my worst enemy had to keep his belongings in a rucksack' because she could never find anything without emptying all her belongings on her bunk. For some time she took up with a nice Italian man, but later teamed up with a Viennese Jew and, after the war, settled in Israel.

The Estonian was called Frau Faust and had a girl of 11 and a boy of nine. She was a very fat lady who, through marriage, had acquired a German passport, which made her an enemy alien. She could speak only Estonian, as she was from a rural part of the country. Luckily, she was very practical and expert at lighting and stoking our stove. She kept us from being very cold through that winter.

Frau Faust was so fat when she arrived that we all assumed that she was heavily pregnant. We were wrong, and after about 18 months she had become very thin and suffered terribly from hunger. To help, she chose to work at night in the kitchen peeling potatoes which would earn her a little extra food. One day there was a terrible snowstorm and the men had to dig little paths from the huts to the kitchen. I was young and strong and thus offered to accompany Frau Faust to the kitchen in the raging storm. We wrapped ourselves up well and fought our way through the blizzard. It was pitch dark, the driving snow provided no visibility and the bitter wind took our breath away. However, we made it to the kitchen. As I started back for my hut I suddenly felt myself sinking deeper and deeper into the snow. I was in up to my waist and could not move. I couldn't see the guiding light in

Surviving the Nazis, Exile and Siberia

the window of my hut. I was blinded by snow and the razor sharp cold wind cut my breath away. I felt desperate. I decided to throw myself flat into the snow and force my legs up free. I gradually succeeded and started to crawl on all fours to distribute my weight. Eventually I saw the light in the hut window and crawled home. Next morning, when the blizzard had abated, I examined what had happened. The men had built a snow wall to protect the path to the kitchen and I had missed the path and went straight into the loose drift on the wrong side of the wall. The snow was so deep there that my short journey could have ended in tragedy. I had much more respect for deep snow from then onwards.

Kok U Sek was built on an abandoned copper mine and smelter. The inside camp, where we were housed, had a guard-house at the gate, which was opened only to let work brigades in and out. Outside the camp fence there were vegetable stores, greenhouses, a large administrative complex and a bakery which provided fresh bread for the camp each morning. Further out there were farms with pigs, cattle and horses. The area around the camp was hilly and in summer was covered in short lush grass. At the bottom of the hill a little brook ran past the bathhouse and on top of the hill there was a piece of rail suspended from a high frame. When hit hard with a hammer the sound could be heard throughout the camp. It was used for the wake-up call and the signal for lights-out. All the huts and barracks were built of *samans* (those clay and straw bricks) and had wooden doors, window frames and trusses. The roofing was made of twigs, similar to gorse and made watertight with clay.

All through the long cold season fuel was a continual need. As wood was scarce and a luxury for carpentry purposes only, we were restricted to extracting fuel from the slag heaps left there by the copper mine. The slag had to be riddled and the usable material only glowed but never gave a flame. It took

Kok U Sek Camp, Karaganda: January 1943–May 1945

the skill of Frau Faust to ensure reasonable heating.

In many ways, my family was better off than the majority of prisoners in the camp. This all stemmed from the tolerance of the secret police officer in Tallinn who had allowed us to bring so much luggage to the first camp at Harju. We had packed virtually a whole household and even our coats played a key part in our survival. Kurt had taken his leather coat which was a necessity in the cold, as it had a camel-hair lining. It ended up being made into a hold-all after the war, when luggage was impossible to buy! I had brought my grandmother's elegant fur coat, which she had given me as a farewell present. I used it as a bed cover on freezing nights but, sadly, after about two years it fell to pieces.

There was a thriving barter system in the camp. We could obtain extra bread or sugar in exchange for a shirt or a towel. I also bartered for shoes for my growing children and later, when we moved to a larger room, I bartered for a table and chairs from the carpenter so that we could eat in a civilised way instead of sitting at the end of our bunks and balancing our bowls. Because we were banned from buying anything from outside the camp we utilised old items as best we could. We got sewing thread from worn-out socks and precious zips and buttons were all saved. The thing I missed most was elastic for knickers because string or buttons create problems in the arctic winter conditions, when fingers are numb from frost. The other main problems were shoes and summer dresses. Shoes issued by the camp were made from old rubber tyres and were incredibly uncomfortable. Summer dresses were a challenge. We needed a new dress each year because after wearing one all through a summer it was practically burnt off your back by the scorching sun. At first it was the fashion to make the dress from men's striped pyjamas, which provided a neat shirt dress. The following year we made dirndl-style dresses from checked tablecloths or used white sheeting with coloured piping.

Looking back in later years I concluded that we internees were better off than the majority of people in Siberia living outside the camps. The 'free' people could only qualify for food rations if they had a job and then, after work, had to queue endlessly for the little that was available to buy. In contrast, we were guaranteed bread and two warm meals every day. In Kok U Sek the daily diet was much like previous camps. In the morning we got a chunk of bread and substitute tea. At lunch we got gruel or watery soup and possibly some salted fish and at night got another bowl of gruel. The gruel was made from millet or oats or some other cereal cooked in water. Usually the gruel remained the same for weeks until the next cereal delivery to the camp. To sweeten our day we got one teaspoonful of sugar. However, come snow-storm or summer drought, the Soviet authorities never failed to feed us.

With all my experience of camp life to that point, I concluded that the hardest part of being a prisoner was not the loss of freedom or being forced to be in a group all the time but the fact that all decisions were made for you by someone else and without any prior warning. This depersonalised you through being stripped of any freedom of choice. It was all-embracing – when, how and where to travel or go; how to be housed; when, what and where to eat; when to wash or have a bath; when, what and where to work; when to get up and when to go to sleep. These are all assumed as automatic choices when you are free; in camp all choice is abruptly withdrawn from you.

But opposing all those negative aspects, we had the advantages of having a roof over our heads, a minimum of food, clothing and medical attention. Conditions were extremely tough in comparison to the central European standards we were used to when growing up in Vienna but better than many millions caught up in the theatre of the World War, further west from us. I was sure that our guards did not see any problems with our position. They did not

Kok U Sek Camp, Karaganda: January 1943–May 1945

know anything better and had no patience with what they perceived as paltry complaints in the middle of wartime conditions. At the time I confronted the commandant in the camp at Aktyubinsk about getting Walter back from hospital he commented, 'Don't you know there is a war going on? I don't know where my wife and children are.'

When the children were old enough to go to the camp nursery, run by two internees, I went to work in the laundry. I had asked to be excused work outside the camp because I needed to stay near my children. The laundry had the advantage that I could occasionally give the children a proper bath. Due to my type of work I was issued an old pair of military boots which became my pride and joy. A simple way to keep them clean was spit and polish. For a more professional job I could mix soap with the soot from a *kaptilka*, a little home-made kerosene lamp consisting of a jar and a metal tube with a wick inside. The wick was most likely cotton stuffing out of a *fufaika*. This is the usual Russian cotton jacket which goes with padded trousers that are held up with string.

The work consisted of washing 30 items each day, mostly sheets and very dirty work-shirts. At times there was no hot water; at other times there was no soap. But, I had to make the best of it. The most difficult part of my job was hanging out the washing in winter. It would often be frozen stiff before I got it up on to the line. My boss in the laundry was a professional laundry worker. He taught me how to wring out large sheets and blankets with minimum energy and maximum effect. I used this method successfully until I got an automatic washing machine many years later.

One day I was ordered to go outside the camp to whitewash a house. I thought it would be fun and was glad to go. I attacked the job with gusto but ended up with blisters all over my hand. I had to use unslaked lime (calcium oxide) and not paint.

Although I cannot remember when it took place, I recall an incident when a medical commission came to examine the fitness of women for work. It was a most embarrassing and humiliating experience. We had to pass in single file, stripped to the waist, past the two doctors who checked and prodded us like cattle in a market. Luckily it happened only once.

The camp authorities made good use of all the skills available amongst the prisoners. The Viennese dentist and doctor had to care for the prisoners and for all the Russian administrative staff. The early days were difficult for the two men, as there were very few instruments or drugs available and no anaesthetics. An agronomist and a veterinary surgeon looked after the farms. Carpenters and masons put up new buildings and the smiths and cobblers were always busy. Dressmakers worked for the wives of the Soviet officers. A school for 30 children was set up by a teacher and a nursery for the pre-school group. Ruth attended the camp school for two years and obtained very good marks which gave her a great boost. Due to a shortage of books and paper, the children were taught arithmetic and writing on little wooden boards, using pencils. After the teacher had seen their homework the boards were scraped clean with a piece of glass, ready to be used again. A group of Spanish sailors, very skilled at macramé, produced sandal uppers, belts and bags in a workshop and I assumed these products were sold by the camp administration at a profit.

My friend Herta had now got over her husband's death in the brickworks in summer 1942 and was very happy to be reunited with her mother. She volunteered for work in the kitchen because she reckoned the extra food was the best she could do for her daughter and her mother. Shortly after joining the kitchen staff, Herta fell in love with the chef, who had his own living quarters because his job was judged so important. Herta and mother and daughter moved into the chef's quarters. I never understood how this sophisticated

Kok U Sek Camp, Karaganda: January 1943–May 1945

woman, whose late husband was a mild-mannered and cultured musician, could fall for this uncouth Italian engine-driver turned cook. I assumed it must be the attraction of opposites!

The authorities had ways of turning a blind eye to a little self-help by prisoners. They must have known that the small vegetable patches, which appeared behind the barracks, were started with seeds and seedlings taken from their nurseries outside the camp. Some people grew carrots and beetroot; others grew cabbages and tomatoes. Some men wanted to grow tobacco only. It was a large leafed variety which, when fully grown, was dried in the sun and its leaves and stalks chopped into fine pieces. A funnel of newspaper was filled with the tobacco to make a cigarette.

One day a very excited woman came to me and said, 'You must punish Walter very severely because he has stolen a carrot from my garden!' The poor little fellow had indeed pulled a carrot from her patch – what a crime! I was extremely annoyed with this woman, who was actually in charge of the nursery school. Since her own little boy had died during the first year of our internment, I would have expected a bit more understanding. Of course, I gave Walter a good ticking off and told him never to do that again.

The main crops in the fields were tomatoes, potatoes, cabbages, carrots, onions and *machorka* – a coarse type of tobacco. The women worked in the fields in the short hot summer and early autumn. For the rest of the year they were busy in the storerooms constantly sifting and moving the stock of vegetables to preserve as many as possible. Men without any specific trade or skill worked on the dam of the reservoir which held melted snow water. During summer the network of canals, fed by the reservoir, was opened and closed by the men to irrigate the various fields. In autumn everyone had to work as required to harvest the various crops.

Surviving the Nazis, Exile and Siberia

The climate was typically mid-continental with freezing winters and very hot summers. Winter brought severe frost and many snowstorms, with temperatures often at –40°C. The summer was short with temperatures of up to and over 40°C. Summer often brought problems. One year the brook at the bottom of the camp dried up, leaving no water for the bathhouse. Wearing sandals made my feet so encrusted with dirt that I thought I might never get them properly clean again. Another summer saw a plague of locusts descend on the area, causing the men to spend hours chasing them away by waving blankets and making a lot of noise. Once, a mud-rain fell on the camp, leaving everything in a terrible mess. It must have originated in a desert storm. The crops grew very fast and everything had to be harvested by mid-September. I believe that climate was very healthy because we had a relatively high survival rate in difficult conditions. The air was clear and dry. The night sky was so clear that you felt you could reach out and almost touch the bright stars. It often struck me that my dear mother in far-off England could see the very same stars.

During the early part of the 1943–44 winter, Kurt was assigned to work on the reservoir dam. Shortly after starting he returned home from work one day suffering from snow blindness. This was a very frightening experience, particularly as there was no cure or treatment for it. Only time could restore his sight. Luckily he was able to see after a few days. He was then put back on to his regular work as a herdsman. The oxen which worked the fields during the summer days had to be driven each night to the mountains to graze and brought back down each morning. In winter the oxen were stockaded. Often Kurt could hear the howling of the hungry wolf packs.

Over the years the camp was almost entirely rebuilt. By the middle of 1944 a new kitchen, a new hospital and a large

Kok U Sek Camp, Karaganda: January 1943–May 1945

house for mothers and children had been built. The house contained rooms, each of which housed two or three mothers, depending on the number of children. Although the rooms had earth floors which had to be washed daily to keep down the dust, they were a great improvement on the tiny hut in which we had huddled before. There was a long central corridor with about eight rooms on each side. Each two rooms were heated by one stove, which was stoked from the corridor. This saved on both labour and fuel, and avoided any mess in the rooms, each of which had a small cooking surface which was also useful for heating water. We all thought the new set-up was luxury itself. Even the dreaded roll-call was discontinued to everyone's relief.

The barracks were spring-cleaned once a year. Everything was brought outside. The walls were whitewashed, the bunks scrubbed in the yard, the straw changed in the mattresses and the sheets laundered. All was dry by evening and returned inside.

Twice each year we had the ritual of the *'obysk'* – the search. These, we were told, took place not only in all Soviet camps and prisons but also in all factories throughout the country. The first *obysk* took place before May Day and the second before the anniversary of the Revolution in November. The search is carried out for hidden weapons. We, of course, had none but occasionally the guards would temporarily confiscate knives, knitting needles and scissors, which we needed for our work duties. To create a festive appearance for May Day some of the artistic men were directed to create mosaics from coloured stones, to look like flower beds.

In January 1944 I collapsed from severe back pains while working in the laundry. When I got home the pain got worse and I was losing what seemed like a bucket of blood. Kurt fetched the medical orderly from the first aid station, who diagnosed a miscarriage. This news came as a great shock.

Surviving the Nazis, Exile and Siberia

Kurt and I never expected that I could become pregnant because, like most other women in the camps, my periods stopped shortly after I was first interned. I received some medicine from the orderly and was told to rest at once. I recovered quickly and was back at work in the laundry after two days. Then the pains returned. I then had a great piece of good fortune because a lady gynaecologist was at that time carrying out a camp visit. She examined me right away and said she would have to perform a small operation. I had to walk to Spaski Camp because the medical facilities were superior there. I was given a pill to calm my nerves as no pain-killers or anaesthetics were available. The operation involved the most excruciating pain, which I would not wish on my worst enemy. I can't bear to focus on it, even after all these years. I was allowed a short rest of only about 15 minutes and then ordered to walk back to Kok U Sek. I walked the half-hour journey slowly by myself. If someone else had described this event, I would never have believed it. When I arrived back I had to pinch myself to confirm that I had lived through the horrific ordeal.

All through 1943 we were told of the Soviet successes in the war and that in January 1944 the Red Army had crossed into Poland, broken through the siege lines at Leningrad and won a major battle at Kiev. The tide was turning. Then in spring 1944 we received our first food aid, donated by the United States. The gift contained cooking oil, egg powder, fish powder, preserves and lots of other items which I cannot remember. It created tremendous excitement and jubilation amongst us and we felt it was an omen that our time of detention may not last many more months. The cooks did their utmost to prepare exotic and tasty dishes which made eating a pleasure for the first time in years. Everyone's health and mood improved suddenly, and there was even more encouraging news from the front. The Soviet army was

Kok U Sek Camp, Karaganda: January 1943–May 1945

powering through the Crimea and had captured its capital, Simferopol. As the weeks progressed we heard of the Allied invasion of Europe and by the end of August we were told of the liberation of Paris. Our optimism seemed justified as the Germans were in retreat on all fronts. The general regimen in the camp reflected this mood and became more relaxed.

Occasionally the camp was given an inspection by higher authorities, even at this time of euphoria. When an inspection was due, the order, *mascirovats* was issued – in other words, hide everything ugly and tidy up. We would get gauze from the infirmary to make curtains. We dyed them cream using onion skins or purple using some tincture from the first aid station. It always reminded me of the well-known 'Potemkin's Villages' of Tsarist times – all show and nothing behind.

About this time some babies were expected. Our new hospital building had been completed at the right time. In the first year, when two babies were born, the authorities moaned and said they were not going to play nursemaid for our children. Now they were very generous. As soon as a doctor confirmed a pregnancy the mother was excused work duties and received children's rations on top of her own allowance. When the baby was born, a cot, a wooden tub and ten yards of muslin for nappies were issued to the mother. Amazingly, some couples, who had given up hope before the war of having a family, found they were going to be parents. Both Herta and I joined the expectant mothers and her son and my daughter were born in the winter of 1944–45. By the time we were all repatriated in 1947 over 50 babies had been born at Kok U Sek.

It was a bitterly cold night in February 1945 when my third child was born. I was then sharing a room with Bella, a teacher, who had a four-year-old son. I lingered as long as possible in the warm bed, delaying my inevitable walk to the hospital in the dark freezing night. When I realised that the contractions were becoming critical, I wakened Bella to get help. She in turn wakened the doctor who was very annoyed at being disturbed at this unsocial hour. Bella then accompanied me to the hospital where, a short time later, the doctor and nurse arrived and told me to 'hold back' as they weren't ready to receive the baby. I tried to comply and, in the end, all was well. I became the delighted mother of a little girl, whom we were to call Leah. I was kept in a private room for two weeks whilst Kurt had to cope with Ruth and Walter who by then were lively seven- and five-year olds respectively. Walter threw a tantrum when he heard he had another sister: he had made a wish to get a baby brother!

Fortunately, I was able to breastfeed little Leah and she developed well. Once when I had a high fever from malaria I did not call the doctor because I was afraid the bitter pills, called Agrichim, that he would prescribe would ruin my milk. They were very effective but made everything yellow. However, when I passed out I had let poor Leah drop to the floor. After that, I realised I needed medical help. Then, when I started to wean her, she suffered from constant diarrhoea which continued no matter what I tried, such as rice-water or a gruel of potato starch without sugar. As there was no fruit available I sometimes fed her fresh carrot juice from carrots which Kurt had pinched during his night duty herding the cattle. Interestingly, the condition stopped immediately after we left the camp in January 1947. Was it the high altitude or the water supply that had caused it? It remained a mystery.

Although I was excused work duties, my time was fully occupied. To keep three growing children fed, clean and clothed is a full-time job, particularly with limited facilities and a whole range of rules and restrictions. Keeping them in clothes meant a lot of re-knitting and the re-shaping of adult garments. It was interesting to observe that women from very simple backgrounds endeavoured continuously to upgrade their families' living standards within the limits imposed by camp life. I admired them all greatly. It is rather ironic to think

Kok U Sek Camp, Karaganda: January 1943–May 1945

that I had brought *Jardin des Modes pour les Enfants*, the French fashion magazine for children, into the camp. I was very friendly with the lady who worked in the sewing room and together we discussed which styles to use for my children. One of my dressing gowns was transformed into a training suit for Walter. Out of two large soft dusters we made a warm winter dress for Ruth. One winter I sacrificed my lovely camel-hair coat to have it transformed into a coat and hat for Ruth, complete with fur trimming. It was a frosty snowy day when she was first allowed to wear the new outfit. She came home with large black stains of axle grease on the lovely coat! She had got them from hanging on to the back of a cart. Apart from the stains she could have been injured if she had fallen off. I was furious. Poor Ruth got her first and last smacking. Her daring adventure had gone badly wrong.

For a time one of my room-mates was a young woman called Emmy. Her husband, like Herta's, had died in 1942 in the brickworks. She now had a little son whose father was her Spanish boyfriend. Emmy was a constant moaner and hypochondriac who was always 'crying wolf'. One night she started groaning and said she felt so bad that she thought she was dying. I didn't pay much attention until she insisted that she was unable to move her hands or her feet. This alarmed me. I ran to get a doctor who came and diagnosed food poisoning at once. He rushed her into the hospital and saved her life by pumping out her stomach.

Generally, in the camp, each ethnic group kept together. Naturally, everyone feels more comfortable with people who share the same language or cultural heritage or ideals. However, there was never any animosity, not even any anti-Semitism, in all the time we were interned in the various camps.

On the other hand, some crossings of the ethnic divides took place. There were many unattached young men – Polish soldiers, Spanish airmen and Spanish sailors – who had no difficulty attracting young single girls, and some married women, as their girlfriends. These liaisons created a few dramas. One in particular sticks in my memory. It concerned Irma, who had German parents but was brought up in Moscow. She arrived in the camp with a little daughter and soon befriended a Polish soldier and had a son by him. One day a high-ranking soldier arrived and asked for Irma. It was her Russian husband. When he discovered her conduct in the camp he didn't even want to see his own daughter and left the camp at once.

Usually I do not like to make sweeping generalisations about particular nationalities because I believe there are good and bad people in each one. But, because we were imprisoned in a sort of glasshouse environment with many nationalities, it was impossible not to notice certain characteristics. The Finns, for instance, were scrupulously clean, taciturn and hard-working. The Spaniards were very loquacious and clever at working at handcrafts. The Poles were extremely conscientious, versatile and diligent at their various trades. The Romanians had a deserved reputation for deviousness. Of course, as always, there were exceptions. Some people created lasting impressions – like my Polish medical orderly, who had probably saved Walter's life with the blood transfusions. Another exceptional man was a middle-aged German who had been a freedom fighter in the Spanish Civil War against Franco. He worked in the kitchen preparing the children's food and even refrained from tasting it so as not to take any away from them. I did not know why he was in the camp and later lost track of him. Also there were Yugoslav boatmen captured on the Danube, Swedish and Danish sailors taken on the North Sea and Spanish sailors captured on the Black Sea. Another group were Austrian and German engineers who were working on contracts in Persia when the Russians overran the country. There was also a

Kok U Sek Camp, Karaganda: January 1943–May 1945

large contingent of Polish soldiers but we did not know why they were there.

All the Jews were political refugees like ourselves. Amongst them were a few ultra-orthodox religious families. Some went so far as to avoid what little meat was available because it was not kosher. We all tried to commemorate our feast days and carry out our annual fast. One year I did not carry out the annual fast as I reckoned I had been fasting all the time. However I felt guilty for some time afterwards as I felt the fast and feast days created an invisible link with my mother. We did have one great disappointment. One autumn the Jews did a deal with the commandant to work their days off so as to have a free day on Yom Kippur, the most sacred of our feasts, the Day of Atonement. Sadly, when the day came around they were sent out to work, in clear breach of the agreed deal.

In May 1945 the end of the war in Europe was broadcast through the loudspeakers, which by now were installed above the large barracks building. Naturally we were jubilant and expected to be released very soon.

Sadly our expectations were dashed. We were repeatedly told over a period of months that there was no rolling stock available to send east and thus the first transports did not start until mid 1946, over a year after the end of the war. The turn of the Austrians and Hungarians came in January 1947 and so we were held captive for almost 21 months after VE Day. A lot more happened in that period.

15 · Post-war Detention: Kok U Sek Camp: May 1945– January 1947

The neighbouring Spaski Camp was, by now, full of German prisoners-of-war. They did not have to work and received much better food than we did or what the local free population could afford. It seems incredible that the Soviet authorities were so lenient with the Germans at that time, given the Nazi atrocities all over Eastern Europe. One can only assume that the Red Army had been too preoccupied with battles to notice what the Germans really got up to.

The German prisoners-of-war once staged a production of a revue, to which we were all invited. It was a most enjoyable evening. In retrospect I shudder when I think of us mingling with Nazi troops, some of whom may have taken part in extermination gangs and most of whom probably were fully in agreement with the Holocaust. Artistes from our camp, under the direction of Herta, staged a musical in which she had been a hit in Riga some years ago. It was called, *Why Do You Tell Lies, Cherie?* and Herta, of course, played the lead. It was a great success and for weeks we were humming the catchy tunes.

On rare occasions we were taken to see a Russian film in the POW camp. One film sticks in my mind because it was utterly unsuitable to be shown to us. It was about a women's prison which was full of corruption and told the story of how a male prisoner bribed his way in to visit his lover. Most other

Post-war Detention, Kok U Camp: May 1945–January 1947

films were propagandist and often showed how corrupt the lives of the aristocracy and the bourgeoisie were before the ideal communist regime took over!

In May 1946, about a year after the end of the war, a decree was issued. It was like a bolt from the blue. All able-bodied men were to be transported from the camp to work in the coal mines near Karaganda. This was unheard of and completely against international conventions. The Soviet government presumably saw an opportunity to use the remaining internees in all their camps as slave labour. The war, of course, had created severe manpower shortages. A number of men, including Kurt, objected and went on hunger-strike. Kurt refused to be separated from his family and the authorities relented; he was not sent away. Three weeks later the men came back, sick and broken. A great friend, Dr Prenzlau, who had been my English tutor in the camp, was hospitalised for over two months.

The scene that Dr Prenzlau described was straight out of hell. The brigade leaders in the mines were sadistic criminals who drove the weak men to work ever faster and harder. There were many accidents involving coal wagons, and injuries were never properly seen to. Sleeping quarters were crude and inadequate; food was distributed in an unjust way with the watery top for the 'foreigners' and the thick contents at the bottom for the crooks. Dr Prenzlau had never done physical work before; he was always detailed to teaching. He was completely unsuited to the physical extremes of coal-mining and it came near to killing him.

In the end we were told that the whole episode had been 'an administrative error'.

As the war was officially over I decided to write letters again. They were smuggled out of the camp and mailed by men whose work took them into Karaganda each day.

My first letter was to mother, whom I hoped was still alive and, if so, would probably be living somewhere in London. As I assumed she was unlikely to reside at her pre-war address, I sent the letter to her at the Jewish Refugee Committee, Woburn House, WC1. After our return to Europe in 1947 I learnt what had happened to my letter. Lotte, my sister, had gone to Woburn House to notify the committee of her change of address. When she was about to leave, one of the staff called her back and said, 'By the way, we have a letter here for your mother.' Lotte couldn't believe it when she recognised my handwriting. Mother didn't believe Lotte's phone call and, only after she got the letter, was she overcome with joy and truly surprised. In London they both were aware of the fate of most of the Jews in Europe and thus had given up hope of ever seeing us again. Mother already had trees planted in Israel in our memory. Now she had so much to look forward to, particularly the grandchildren she had never seen.

Mother and Lotte both wrote replies, but they never reached us in the camp. The same happened to a parcel sent from London by cousin Gertrude. However we did receive our only parcel from my Aunt Joan in Shanghai. Aunt Joan and her husband had arrived in Shanghai aboard the last boat leaving Europe for the Far East before the war. There were thousands of refugees living in Shanghai's international zone but later, under Japanese occupation, they were herded into a ghetto. Mother had written to her telling her of the joyous news of our survival and Aunt Joan very kindly sent us many gifts in her parcel. She got to the United States ahead of the communist takeover of China. Her husband had died in China of a tropical disease.

My second letter was to Berta Itskovits, the daughter of our great friends in Tallinn who had been so helpful to us and who had been the proxy grandparents to our children for the three years we spent in Estonia. I wrote to their apartment

Post-war Detention, Kok U Camp: May 1945–January 1947

block, which had been Berta's pre-war address. A few weeks later one of the internees who worked in the administration block outside the camp handed me a letter and said, 'I picked this out of the wastepaper basket.' If it had not been for his alertness and kindness I would never again have got into contact with my dear friend from Tallinn. There was no point in complaining about the handling of the mail; there was never any rational explanation given by the authorities for any of their actions.

Berta had been evacuated from her apartment in 1941 but had returned to it in recent times. Luckily her husband and two brothers survived the war and had spent most of it serving in the Red Army. This was unusual in Tallinn. Most women had returned but very few men survived the war years. She informed me that her mother was alive and well but that her father had starved to death in late 1941. I still remember him as he was – our kind, cultured benefactor.

When our friend Dr Prenzlau had recovered sufficiently from his horrific ordeal in the coal mines, I decided to give him a treat and celebrate his birthday in style. Although he looked haggard and aged, it was only his 46th birthday. I asked an internee who worked on the farm outside to try to get me some meat. The best he could get were ram's testicles! This challenged my creativity, but I managed a tasty dish by using a mix of vegetables. At least it was much better than serving *'suslik'*, a kind of fieldmouse, which we ate occasionally. I brought a tablecloth and proper plates from our suitcases in the storeroom to give the meal a festive feel. This was one of the few happy memories Dr Prenzlau had during all his years in the camps.

Dr Prenzlau (Fritz) had been special to us and we were in the camps with him all through the war. We had met him on the first day of our internment in our first camp, at Harju in Estonia. During 1945 and part of 1946 I had regular English conversation lessons with him. He also taught classical subjects to a number of teenage boys in the camp and enabled them to proceed with academic studies very soon after their release. He had come originally from Hamburg and was returned there in 1946. He then settled in Sweden with his new wife, Topsi, and we visited them in Stockholm in the post-war years. He remarried because his first wife, an Estonian, had disowned him, to his great sorrow. Topsi and Fritz visited us in Kilkeel in 1975 and we exchanged correspondence and gifts until Fritz's death in 1980.

As we entered 1946 the camp regimen remained as before, although there was a growing level of barter amongst us which brought a higher level of ingenuity in trading practices. Tobacco and paper for making cigarettes remained key scarce currencies. There was a constant shortage of both and a growing demand. Anyone who owned a newspaper or book would 'sell' it in cigarette size bits for a good profit. One man, who owned a copy of *Gone with the Wind*, hit the jackpot and was reckoned to be our 'richest' internee. As usual there were no matches so the smoker used either a magnifying glass in bright sunshine to ignite the cigarette or ignite tinder by striking a flintstone with an iron bar. I was a smoker at that time and had my own tinderbox, flint and iron. To light the stove fire we had to go to the smithy and beg for a bucketful of glowing embers.

The Soviet Union entered the war against Japan in August 1945 and, by spring 1946, Japanese prisoners-of-war arrived at the neighbouring Spaski camp. By then the Germans had been moved west. The Japanese prisoners were made to work by the Soviet authorities and, as they moved around the area, looked pathetic in their shabby uniforms. They were badly fed and their constant hunger drove them to exchange their meagre belongings for bread. Often they would offer their gym-shoes, which had a separated big toe. When the children

Post-war Detention, Kok U Camp: May 1945–January 1947

saw these shoes they screamed in terror as they imagined that they were worn by some devil or demon. Other items they frequently exchanged were beautiful long vests and long underpants both made of a silk and wool blend. They had no idea how cold the arctic winter would be.

On 8 June, I celebrated my 30th birthday with a very low-key party, which included the family, the others in my hut and a few friends of Kurt. The meal comprised our ordinary rations supplemented by some fruits and vegetables smuggled in by internees from the stores. A birthday cake was made from soaked white bread, baked crushed beetroot and sugar. I enjoyed being the centre of attention and receiving a few simple gifts. Each adult had to perform a party piece. More than 50 years later it all seems to be another world. Looking back and comparing life today, I am amazed at the variety and depth of experience I had by that early age. It was enough to fill a few lifetimes.

Anticipating our release, I decided to knit complete outfits for each of the three children, a pullover for Kurt and a cardigan for myself. My source of yarn was the Japanese underwear. I couldn't get enough of it. I first took out all the seams very carefully, then unravelled the knitting and finally put the yarn into hanks. I had to wash the hanks carefully to get all the crinkles out. I then knitted the garments, using some coloured yarn I had in my possession to ornament the monotonous army beige. Each of the children got a cap, a scarf, mittens, a pullover and a pair of trousers. I knitted the two garments for Kurt and myself and I still have the cardigan, which is nearly in as good condition now as it was over 50 years ago.

In the autumn of 1946 I had two dreams. They stayed in my mind for many years. In the first dream I found myself in a large city, the likes of which I had never seen before. It was full of bleak concrete skyscrapers. There were streets and streets full of them. It must have been the New York of my imagination, influenced by what I had read about years before. In the second dream I was standing in a wool shop in Vienna – very like the one mother owned until 1938. I was going to create fabulous knitwear designs for our family friend, Bernhard Altmann, who had been a major knitwear manufacturer. When I had this dream, cut off from the outside world for many years, I had no way of knowing whether he was alive or where he was. Amazingly, Bernhard got me started in my own knitwear manufacturing business in 1949.

Extraordinary circumstances often throw up extraordinary deeds and extraordinary people, some of whom I have mentioned. Another of these was Ljuba. I remember her particularly because of the fashion show in summer 1946 that she put on for a few friends.

Ljuba and her three-year-old daughter had been arrested in Moscow with barely a change of clothes in her possession. She had grown up in Moscow, but had a Viennese mother and so had retained German nationality. Ljuba had two main ambitions. One was never to have to work and the other was to acquire a wardrobe of very good Western clothes. She developed a wonderful expertise at working all the systems.

In her early days in the camp she had a romantic liaison with a Czech man. He soon had to leave because, like all the young Czech men, he was drafted into the Czech Volunteer Force and sent west. In due course she gave birth to their baby girl. She received every help and support from my French friend, Jeanne and Jeanne's twin children, a girl and boy of seven. Jeanne and Ljuba had managed to stay together as bunk neighbours throughout all the years of our internment.

Ljuba soon found herself a new boyfriend. He was a very jovial Romanian and, as before, Ljuba gave birth to another

Post-war Detention, Kok U Camp: May 1945–January 1947

baby girl. Thus she effectively achieved her ambition to avoid having to go out to work.

Her second ambition to amass Western clothes was assisted by her increased family. She now was entitled to enough surplus food to enable her to barter for her chosen items. She was successful enough to be able to put on her own fashion show. She looked very elegant in the dresses, coats and even furs which she had amassed over the years.

After the war I heard the next few episodes in Ljuba's story. She ended up in Vienna but decided to return to the camp to obtain the release of her Romanian boyfriend. This was categorically refused by the Soviets and so she had to give up and return to Vienna. There she found a very wealthy widower whom she married. The penniless waif from Moscow had arrived!

At last, in January 1947, it was the turn of us Austrians and the Hungarians to be released and to begin the long journey home. Most of the people in this group were Jewish.

16 · The Long Trek Home, Karaganda to Vienna: January–March 1947

Like most January days, 26 January 1947 was clear and frosty. None of the 200 internees boarding the open lorries would have cared much if the weather had been inclement. We were being set free and on our way back to our beloved Austria and Vienna.

The lorries took about an hour to get from Kok U Sek to a prisoner-of-war camp just outside Karaganda. My only worry was for two-year-old Leah. Luckily she was already potty-trained; if she had wet herself her clothes would have frozen stiff very quickly. Such are the hazards of child-rearing in such a hard climate. When we arrived at the camp we were ushered into an assembly hall and had to settle on the floor. Walter, who was an inquisitive and independent child, set off to scout the area. On his return, he reported that he had been to the coal mines! I never found out whether that was true or not.

The next day we were allowed to go unescorted to a market in Karaganda. I had selected a few items from our meagre possessions to exchange in the market – some plates, a bag and an umbrella. There was no problem exchanging these Western goods. It was very amusing and fascinating to watch all the strange characters as they haggled, bought and sold. One man approached Kurt, grabbed at his leather coat and asked, 'How much do you want for this?' Of course, it

The Long Trek Home, Karaganda to Vienna: January–March 1947

wasn't for sale. The Kasakhs who came in to the market from the rural areas all wore their traditional clothing – floor-length fur coats, fur-lined pointed hats and fur-lined boots. Their dark Mongolian looks appeared intimidating but they were really a friendly people. We ended up with provisions – sugar, sausages and some kind of rolls.

The following day we were notified that our train was ready and we were led to the railway station at Karaganda where the inevitable cattle trucks awaited us. The men were advised to steal as much coal as possible to stow under the bunks to ensure some heating on the journey. They acquired a reasonable supply. We set off in the early afternoon and immediately noticed a major difference from previous journeys. This time no one was locked up and the accompanying troops were on the train for our protection.

We started our long journey by going north-west through the Kazakh countryside. The winter scene of desolate plains and mountains, enveloped in deep snow, became monotonous after some hours. Winter in central Asia had a sameness about it and lost any attraction after you had suffered through one. Each winter was the same, with its 40 degrees of frost at times and frequent snowstorms. We found out later that the winter of 1947 was the worst in the West for years; in Kazakhstan it was of the same severity as other years – there was no such thing as a good winter there.

The journey proceeded with the customary stops and starts and with the severe jolting of the train that we had suffered on our previous journeys. We were able to keep reasonably warm by using the coal taken before we left Karaganda. After almost six days we arrived in the Russian town of Kartaly, some 700 miles from our starting point. I decided to go to the station shop to see if I could buy some sweets for the children. There was a very long queue at the buffet but a kind stranger bought the sweets for me. When I went back to the platform our train was not there. I had a panic attack. This was my worst nightmare – alone in the middle of the Soviet Union without money and without papers and separated from my family. After asking in my best Russian whether someone could tell me where the train was, I was eventually shown by a station worker where to find it. It had been shunted into a siding. I would be more aware in the future!

We then turned west and began the long journey across Russia and the Ukraine. All through this journey there were delays for various reasons. Often we were shunted into a siding to allow troop trains full of soldiers, equipment and booty to pass through. All through the period of our journey we saw many of these trains, which had priority on the railway lines. Many of them were travelling from the West into central Russia with war booty.

We learnt to live as best we could in the cramped conditions and accepted them better than before because of our euphoria at getting home to freedom. The weather got milder as the weeks passed and as we went further west. We got out of the train at any town we stopped in and purchased a few luxuries. From Kartaly we went west through Chkalov and Uralsk and, after some 750 more miles and ten more days, crossed the Volga at Saratov. Here we were taken to a bathhouse in the city, which was a luxury and a great relief after so many days cooped up in our cattle trucks. From there we headed south to Stalingrad, where we could see destruction everywhere and all the detritus of battle as we passed through the outskirts on our way west. After many days of delays and slow travelling we arrived at Dnepropetrovsk, the large Ukrainian city on the River Dnieper. Here again were many signs of the great destruction caused by the war. We could see during our stopover that the people looked quite poor and that they were heavily involved in reconstructing their city.

The Long Trek Home, Karaganda to Vienna: January–March 1947

It took us over four weeks to arrive at Dnepropetrovsk, which meant that we were travelling at around only 70 miles per day. Some of our group estimated that Vienna was over a thousand miles further west and, as the delays were getting more frequent the further we travelled, we could take at least another three weeks to complete our journey. At the time this length of journey in those conditions was, in fact, horrific. However, my memories of our happiness have always diluted those of the deprivations. Nowadays it would be unthinkable to have to live on a cattle truck for two months.

Our journey did, in fact, take an unbelievable 63 days from the time we left the camp at Kok U Sek to when we arrived in Vienna. As we moved further west through the Ukraine, the 400 miles from the Dnieper to the Romanian border town of Iasi took almost ten days. This stretch of track was continuously used by the Red Army as well as civilian services. We were always put at the back of the queue and spent most of our days parked in railway sidings. On arrival at the Romanian border we were told to change into an ordinary passenger train. We took a short ride to where our new cattle trucks were parked. We switched across on to our train which was a narrower gauge European one. The wider gauge Russian rolling stock could only go as far as the Romanian border.

We were allowed a long stop at Iasi. Kurt went into the town to shop and returned with butter and sugar. I whipped this into butter cream to have a belated celebration of Leah's second birthday which had been on 3 February. All the years we were away we had kept a large white British £5 note hidden in a ball of wool. At Iasi we decided to use the £5 to send a telegram to Kurt's parents at their address in Northern Ireland. We composed our message and gave it and the money to a perfect stranger on the platform. The man did send it and it reached its intended destination. This was the first news of our return for any of our relatives in the West.

We then headed across the northern Carpathian mountains to the Romanian border town of Oradea and crossed the border into Hungary. Our guards decided to give us a break from the weeks of travelling and took us for a stopover at a prisoner-of- war camp. To our total dismay the camp was run by the German prisoners. We felt insulted that, after five and a half years in Siberian camps we had fallen into the hands of the Germans. I felt very angry and unhappy, and was glad when our two-day stay was over.

We continued our journey without the Hungarians in our group. They had been set free after our visit to the camp. When we stopped in a small Hungarian town a group of local Jews came to the train to welcome us. When the women saw our children they could not believe their eyes. They all said, 'You still have children! Ours have all been killed by the Nazis.' This was the first time we had come face to face with evidence of the Nazi atrocities. We felt numb and all we could do was comfort these poor mothers. When the Soviet troops had told us about the Nazi atrocities and how the Nazis were exterminating Jews and other groups, we were certain it was Soviet propaganda and did not believe any of it. It seemed too horrific to be possible. Now we knew that something awful had happened.

On arrival in Budapest a huge consignment of food from the American-Jewish aid agencies awaited us. I remember in particular the large quantities of chocolate bars and tins of sardines. There was so much that we shared some of it with our Soviet guards. They could not comprehend how anyone would give food away.

We then moved further west to Gjor where we had to stay for two days on the train because of a delay in clearance into Austria and pressure of traffic on the line. Some of the townspeople invited the children into their homes. Ruth discovered a bathroom for the first time in her life.

Shortly after we left Gjor we crossed the border into

The Long Trek Home, Karaganda to Vienna: January–March 1947

Austria. It is impossible to describe my feelings when our train entered Austrian soil. I could feel the hairs rise on the back of my neck; I started to cry; I hugged Kurt and my beloved children. Everyone was very excited and very emotional. It was too much for one elderly man; he died of a heart attack on the way to Vienna. Then I caught a glimpse of the snow-covered peaks of the Alps in the distance. I couldn't stop crying for joy. 'Now I know we're home at last ', I cried.

We arrived at Vienna station on a Russian cattle train on 29 March 1947 after being over nine weeks in transit from Kazakhstan. The journey had started in the arctic winter and ended in the gentle spring weather of Austria. We were back in the city we had fled some eight and a half years before.

We were taken, with our battered belongings, to a hospital for disinfection, a procedure we knew well from past experience. From there we were taken to a large school, where we were housed. Each classroom had four families. Our children looked remarkably well after their years of ordeals. Ruth was now nine, Walter was seven and little Leah was two.

Although we had no money and no home to go to we were full of optimism. We were confident that one day we would return to a normal life.

17 · Vienna: March–September 1947

Four weeks after settling down in our classroom we received a visitor who was to change our lives miraculously. The elegant lady who came to see us was the personal secretary before the war of our long-standing family friend, Bernhard Altmann. She had come to tell us of Bernhard's kind offer of the use of a fully furnished apartment in the fashionable Hitzing district, which was untouched by the war. (This was amazing, considering the extent of war damage that Vienna had suffered.) The owner, a relation of Bernhard's, had had to flee Vienna some time ago. We could hardly believe our good fortune.

Bernhard had been generous to our family all through the years of his outstanding business success. His flair and entrepreneurial spirit had made him the hero of my youth. He had a personality that made people admire him unconditionally or dislike him as a ruthless type.

My last really fond memory was dancing with him at the Altman factory ball in 1933. In the years to 1938 I rarely met him because of our work commitments and of course from 1938 I had lost all contact. His offer of the apartment confirmed for me the depth of his generosity.

We moved soon into our two-room luxury apartment. The larder was still full of food and there were many household goods left behind when the owners fled abroad. The children

Vienna: March–September 1947

took like ducks to water to the modern bathroom. They had not known such luxury before in their young lives. I was mainly impressed by the miraculous effect of Persil washing powder on all the clothes!

Ruth and Walter went to a local school. Both could speak German, but neither could read or write it. School proved difficult for them because of that, and Ruth would get very upset when the teacher smacked her. I suspected this was uncalled for because Ruth was always a helpful and pleasant child. However, mothers are usually biased!

Shortly after we moved into our new home parcels arrived from mother and Lotte in England and from relations in the United States. Some of these parcels contained second-hand clothes. A friendly seamstress we found transformed some into dresses for the girls and she remodelled men's suits into costumes for me. At that time there was no way of obtaining any new items in Vienna. A particularly welcome parcel arrived from Bernhard in New York. At that time he was very involved with his business interests in America and with rebuilding his business in Europe. We were most appreciative that this busy entrepreneur would take the time to shop at Woolworths and purchase all the toiletries that any family could wish for. All these were either unobtainable or unaffordable in Vienna.

We were also helped greatly by Jewish aid organisations, mostly with clothes for the children and food parcels. Soon our children were better dressed than their classmates, who thought that they were foreigners.

The general situation in Vienna was really dreadful; you could not even buy a spool of sewing thread. Kurt's worn-out leather coat was used to make a very large handbag for me, because suitcases that were on sale were made of cardboard. One way the population tried to overcome all these shortages was by way of barter. In the building of a former department store called Gerngross, was an exchange centre. It worked in the following way: you could take any surplus article there, the value was assessed and you received an appropriate number of coupons. Then you could look around for whatever you needed among the items on offer and use the coupons as payment. The store took a small commission. We received so many parcels from England and America that I was able to use some surplus goods. For example, I acquired a portable Corona typewriter that way, but I had to ask my friends in America to get me a ribbon for it.

While we lived in the school we were given meals there, but as soon as we moved into our own flat I had to cook. Since much of our food aid came in tins, such as coffee, corned beef and fish, I always had a small tin-opener in my purse. Our meals were mostly vegetarian because there was very little meat on sale. Fortunately, Kurt had a cousin who owned a fruit and vegetable wholesale business in the market. She was very generous to our family. I made dumplings, pancakes, spaghetti and the like, as it was essential to give the children rich food because all three of them were much too thin.

Unfortunately, Ruth and Walter again had malaria and tonsilitis, so for a while I had two children in hospital. Leah coughed a lot. The doctor said it was whooping cough but I did not believe him. Six months later it was established in London that she had tuberculosis; she had to rest for a year and that cured her.

We were able to just make ends meet. During the last years in the camp Kurt had worked on an invention for an improvement in radios. It was all in his head, because there was no paper available. As soon as we arrived in Vienna he started to work on his written submission for a patent. He also got in contact with Philips, Eindhoven, to offer his invention. I did all his typing. I had also to type a letter to the British

Vienna: March–September 1947

Embassy regarding our visas. We had to prove that we were refugees, returned from captivity in the Soviet Union and not former Austrian Nazis.

Kurt had also to fulfil another duty. Walter, the teenage son of our seamstress friend from the camp, had been one of Dr Prenzlau's pupils. In order to enter university he had to attend a course and pass an exam. Some vindictive person wanted to jeopardise this, maintaining that mother and son were Nazis who had caused the father's early death in the camp. This was of course a malicious fabrication. We had known the family from the first days in Harju. Kurt vouched for the boy's good character and cleared his name. In the event Walter became one of the youngest history professors at the University of Vienna. He retired in 1996 and is writing his final opus, the history of one of the medieval Polish kings. We are still good friends.

In 1947, while Vienna was under the four-power occupation of the United States, Britain, France and the Soviet Union and divided into four zones, all incoming and outgoing mail was censored. The four powers took turns in their duties of administration and this arrangement lasted for ten years until, in June 1955, Austria became an independent neutral state.

Kurt found part-time work teaching at his old technical school and I was paid a small inheritance from my grandmother's estate. Then one day I decided to visit the Hotel Bristol, my old place of work. The old part of the hotel was bombed out of existence. The new part was being used by the American occupying forces. To my delight I found my former director, Mr Primus, reinstated to his former position. He told me that he and his wife, who was Jewish, had spent the whole war 'underground' – hidden by a non-Jewish friend, an employee of the hotel. The poor man had spent many years living on the edge in mortal danger and I was so happy that he was rewarded after the war with a senior position in the hotel.

Surviving the Nazis, Exile and Siberia

We talked at length about my exile and war years in Estonia and in Kazakhstan, and finally detailed the story of my 1938 court case which awarded me an out-of-court settlement of half of my claim. He listened attentively, thought for a while, and then offered to pay me the other half of my claim. I was flabbergasted and delighted. Now we had the money for our hoped-for passage to the United Kingdom. I made a point of keeping in touch with Director Primus for the rest of his life.

At that time too, it was very difficult to find a cobbler or tailor. They wanted to serve their established customers only, even when you brought your own leather (sent from the United States) or good material. Luckily we had Mrs Leitsch, the seamstress from the camp, who was happy to sew for us. We were also very fortunate to be able to recover some jewellery for my mother-in-law and one of my aunts. Some decent people had hidden it and were delighted to hand it over to us for transport to England. We received many visitors in our cosy home as we were always there in the evenings because of the children.

When Kurt's family had received our telegram from Romania on our way home, they went into action at once to obtain entry permits for us. We planned to join them in Londonderry. We enjoyed our luxurious apartment for almost six months until our permits arrived and we set off in late September 1947 to travel by train and boat to London, nine years after we had left Vienna.

Part 3

Never Say, 'I Can't'; Say, 'I'll Try': 1947–99

18 · London: September–October 1947

When we arrived at London's Waterloo station, mother and Lotte were there to meet us. It was one of the most emotional moments of my life. I could never describe adequately my feelings of joy when I hugged my mother and Lotte on the station's concourse. The significance of the moment was created, not just by our long absence, but by the evidence that we had all survived. We all knew by then how lucky we were to have avoided the fate that befell millions of our fellow Jews. I could see the recognition of this in my mother's eyes. It had been a long nine years for all of us.

Only when I became a grandmother did I really understand my mother's joy at seeing her grandchildren for the first time and the daughter whom she thought she had lost for ever. Some years earlier she had become convinced that we had perished. She had last received a letter from us in 1940, enclosing a photograph of the two children and myself. After almost seven years without news, she had the trees planted in Israel in our memory. Thus, she took some time to absorb the presence and appearance of the children who were bemused at having a grandmother for the first time.

We had received work permits for the firm in Londonderry which made artificial flowers and was part-owned by Robert Sekules, Kurt's brother. The plan, however, was to stay for five weeks in Lotte's London apartment as she was going to move to Cardiff to join her husband. After arriving in London from Vienna in 1938, Lotte spent about a year in domestic service until she was sacked by her employer because she was then an enemy alien. During the war she worked as a turner in a factory and, in 1942, married Ernst Foges, a very distant relation from Gablonz, who had a jewellery and appliqué business. My mother also had entered domestic service after her arrival in England and worked as a cook in private houses. Later she moved to live with father's two cousins, Lise and Martha Mendel, and found employment in the clothing industry.

Lotte told me after the war about one poignant incident during mother's domestic employment. On 5 April 1939 mother received a phone call from Vienna. It was our father who wanted to wish her well on the occasion of their silver wedding anniversary. Mother felt terribly embarrassed by the call and her reaction did not match father's eager tenderness, he later wrote to Lotte. Father never really understood the very strained relationship between the Jewish domestic servants and their rather apprehensive employers. As soon as war broke out mother and Lotte lost their jobs.

We spent our first evening recounting some of our experiences. These chats were to continue for a number of weeks. Mother, ever practical, gave each of us a torch and a hot-water bottle; she believed that they were the most important essentials for safe and comfortable living in post-war London.

Mother insisted that I take Leah to a children's specialist who promptly diagnosed that she had tuberculosis. On the bright side, mother arranged that I could attend a concert conducted by Vaughan Williams in the Maida Vale studio of the BBC. It was my very first encounter with English contemporary music.

I tried to spend as much time as I could with mother, whilst

London: September–October 1947

ensuring I saw as many of London's sights as possible. I feared that once we had landed in the remote and faraway Northern Ireland I would not be able to return! My growing inquisitiveness about our new chosen location caused me a problem. One day I had an accident in an Underground station. Whilst waiting for a train, a poster advertising travel to Northern Ireland attracted my attention. As I walked along the platform to get a closer look, I became so engrossed that I wasn't looking where I walked. I stepped off the platform and fell into the pit on to the rails. A bystander helped me back up and, apart from the shock at being nearly electrocuted, I was none the worse for my fall.

Towards the end of October we went on the last stage of our journey. We took the train to Liverpool, crossed by boat to Belfast and then went by train to Londonderry. We were pleasantly surprised by the tranquility and beauty of the Irish countryside. Perhaps we would find new happiness there.

19 · Londonderry: October 1947–December 1949

I remember well our emotional reunion with Kurt's mother, and that she could not understand that I allowed two-year-old Leah to run around. She thought I should take her by the hand but I was quite confident that she would not get into mischief – maybe I would think differently now.

Kurt's mother was now a widow and we moved in to live with her. My father-in-law had worked as a consultant in Robert's Londonderry firm in the years before his death in 1941. In 1939 the family had rented a house in a Garden City in the outskirts but, after his father had died, Robert and his wife Ellie rented a house opposite the factory. During her widowed years, Mrs Sekules supplemented her pension from Robert by giving piano lessons and by taking in lodgers. Stella, Kurt's sister and the eldest of the three, had disappeared with her two children during the war. Her husband, who survived the war in the Yugoslav army, could not trace them, so we assumed that they had been sent to an extermination camp.

We all settled in well, as my mother-in-law was very welcoming and glad of the company – particularly of her grandchildren. Shortly after our arrival, I was invited by the Rotary Club to address a lunchtime meeting. They were fascinated to hear about our wartime experiences. The subject and my presence were both of great novelty value. The Soviet

Londonderry: October 1947–December 1949

Union was another world for them and I happened to be their first female speaker. I regarded this invitation as a great honour. On the other hand, it presented a tremendous challenge to me – with my 'school' English and only a few weeks of living in the UK. All went well, however, and several local newspapers reported my talk. In later years I was to address the local Dinner Club in Kilkeel and became a regular speaker at Women's Institute gatherings, often up to six times each season. Travel in later years allowed me to add slides about Israel, Hong Kong, Japan, Australia and modern Russia.

The first two years in Londonderry were very tough for us because, for most of the time, Kurt had no job. I got an afternoon job in a toy factory, earning the princely sum of £3 per week. The business was owned by another refugee family and was successful in producing teddy bears and dressed dolls. Each afternoon I stitched as many dolls' rompers as colleagues did in a full day but I didn't take any smoke breaks and refrained from dancing and singing, like the others, during 'Workers' Playtime', the popular daily radio programme. I did not need a work permit, as the immigration officer in England had entered 'Landed Unconditionally' on my passport – perhaps it was my smile! The work hours allowed me to do my housework in the mornings and the money had to feed all of us. Luckily my Siberian experience of vegetable-growing paid off – I used the garden to reduce my shopping bill.

In 1949, well into our second year, we became desperate. We knew the extension of permits for our family would be refused whilst Kurt was unemployed. Under no circumstances would we go back to Austria. We kept mother informed of our dilemma.

Often in life the darkest night turns into the brightest dawn. One day, during our lowest period, a neighbour fetched me to take a telephone call from London. The voice said, 'Edith, how are you?'. It was Bernhard Altmann. I couldn't believe it. As before, and since, Bernhard was to come to our rescue and to earn my eternal admiration and gratitude. My mother must have told him of our plight. He asked, 'Would you consider starting a knitting factory? If you did something to create jobs, you would qualify for an extension of your permits.' I was elated. I told him clearly, 'If you think I can do it, I'll try.' His confidence in my ability opened the way for a new life for all of us. There is no doubt in my mind that, without Bernhard's moral support and encouragement, I could never have developed my business.

By this time, Bernhard had been given back his factory and buildings in Vienna and was in the process of re-equipping his plundered plant and building a major extension. He also had a factory in Texas and an office in New York.

After this telephone conversation the dream I had in the camp in 1946 came back into my mind. At that time I had no idea whether Bernhard was alive and, if so, where he was. In my dream I found myself in Vienna in a wool shop like that of my mother's before the war and producing designs for Bernhard's factory. Oddly enough, another dream at that time had me in a fantastic city full of concrete skyscrapers. Evidently my subconscious was preoccupied with liberation and plans for the future.

I intended to start with sock production and it was agreed that mother and I would go to the machine manufacturers in Leicester and learn how to work the equipment. I reported to the police before crossing to England to spend two weeks on the training course. My only experience was with two knitting needles. I had become expert with them and, in the camp in 1946, I had knitted about 30 items for my family, all from ripped-out yarn. Some of this yarn came from the wool and silk underwear which the Japanese prisoners-of-war had swapped for food. Now I faced a real challenge. I had never

Londonderry: October 1947–December 1949

seen a knitting machine before. Mother watched for two days and then exclaimed, 'Never! I could never learn that!' She returned to London.

Slowly, but surely, I learnt how to master the machine. I was highly motivated because I wanted to prove to Bernhard that I deserved all the confidence he was showing in me. I returned home with my first pair of Argyle socks!

On my return from England to Northern Ireland I had to go through a customs check and show my Austrian passport and my Alien's book. I was very worried that they would not allow me back – I had not yet got over feeling nervous and intimidated by authorities or people in uniform, which stemmed from my experiences of the Gestapo in Vienna and the KGB in the Soviet Union. I felt like this on my two or three journeys each year to London, and I only relaxed after we were granted British citizenship, after living for five years in the United Kingdom.

Whilst I was in Leicester two knitting machines were dispatched to our place in Londonderry. This had been arranged by Bernhard, with payment when I could afford it. Kurt fixed them to a table in our bedroom and he became my first pupil. Everything proved difficult at first. We didn't know we had to oil the new machines and so the speed was very low. It took a whole day to knit one pair of socks. Kurt, a patient pupil, also cut out the pressing shapes and his mother hand-grafted the toes. It was a family business in the literal sense.

Clothing was still on ration coupons in 1949 and only utility goods, with their distinctive label, were available in the shops. All socks were plain grey. We were lucky because wool for handknitting did not require coupons. I bought light grey and oatmeal for the background and many bright colours for the pattern. Soon Kurt and I were producing a dozen pairs each week and I was advised to charge ten shillings (50 pence) for a pair. I thought this an outrageous price because I related it to my weekly income from the toy factory. I went to three of the best men's outfitters in Londonderry and offered the product. The buyers responded very favourably. My first customer was Gieves, the Navy outfitters, who were absolutely delighted to see the first fashion socks since the pre-war years. The other two ordered as well, providing enough work to keep us going. Because I was dedicated to the highest quality, I often felt guilty when I mended a fault invisibly, but I soon came to realise that mending is a normal part of every knitting production.

I reported our progress to Bernhard. He pointed out that I would never get very far by working the machines myself. He said I should obtain premises and train staff to work the machines – he would organise the purchase of more.

I contacted the head of the Department for New Industries at the Ministry of Commerce, who was extremely helpful and gave me a list of six towns that were potentially interested in new types of employment for women.

As I had to travel by train or bus, I could visit only one town each day. The main obstacle was a shortage of suitable premises, which was exacerbated by the strict building restrictions which had remained in place after the war. One town council offered me the town hall, but it turned out they were not allowed to do that, as it had to remain available for public purposes, such as ballroom dances. Afterwards, I read in the paper that this hall had to be closed because the floor was too weak for the new rock-'n-roll craze! Evidently I had had a lucky escape! In another town I was offered an old technical school but I found out it would take six months or more to obtain agreement from all the owners and this was too long to wait. Some other towns had no premises available.

My last trip was the longest of all and was to prove successful. It was to Kilkeel in the south-east of Northern Ireland, the longest distance of any of the towns from

Londonderry: October 1947–December 1949

Londonderry. After the train journey to Belfast I then had a two-hour bus journey to Kilkeel. As usual, I first went to the town clerk, Bertie Cousins, who then introduced me to the chairman of Kilkeel Town Council, Bob Linton. He was very keen to attract industries which would employ women because the town had only work in fishing and granite-quarrying which, in those days, employed only men. He persuaded Mr Graham, the owner of an empty loft above his carpentry shop, to let it to me. It was suitable and eventually I agreed to rent it for five years at £75 per year. I ordered three long strong tables and two dozen stools. We were to move in at the beginning of 1950.

All my travels took place in December 1949, when the short days gave me no chance to see the landscape. I felt I had travelled in darkness to the end of the world. Soon after, I began to enjoy and appreciate the beautiful local countryside with its majestic Mourne mountains and wonderful coastline. Fate had turned out to be kind.

Next, we had to find somewhere to live. Bertie Cousins took me first to his sister's house and then we started our search. In darkness, we tramped over field and clambered over stiles, only to be refused everywhere. Nobody wanted children in their house. We didn't give up and eventually we came to a large house where the young mother agreed to let me two rooms and allowed me to share her kitchen. When I returned with all the good news, Kurt's mother was very sad at the prospect of being left alone again. I assured her that she would live with us, as soon as we had our own house. I had been promised the first finished council house, which was being built at the time.

20 · Kilkeel – The Early Years: 1950–55

I moved with Walter and Leah to Kilkeel on 1 January 1950. Walter was then almost ten and Leah almost five. Ruth and Kurt stayed behind in Londonderry because Ruth had to sit her eleven-plus examination in the spring. She passed, after living for only two years in Northern Ireland. By then, she had forgotten all the Russian she had learnt in the two years in the camp school. At that time we spoke only German at home.

After Kurt and Ruth came to Kilkeel, some weeks later, we started an intensive recruitment drive and a training programme. Twelve machines had been delivered from England and so we started two more girls each week until all the machines were staffed. Kurt was an excellent trainer, although a slow knitter, and was also busy constructing additions to the machines to improve the process. One excellent addition fed elastic thread into the rib-tops of ankle socks. We trained the girls in the evenings outside working hours and found them very quick at grasping the new skills. Although some were as young as fourteen and had come straight from school, they all became fully proficient within a year. They were very pleasant and eager. Most lived in the town and walked home for their lunch. Others travelled in on bicycles. Once they got the hang of the job their confidence reflected in their non-stop talk in their lovely local dialect

Kilkeel – The Early Years: 1950–55

with 'Says I ...' or 'Says she, but ...'. They often sang all the latest hits and a favourite song included the line, 'O Johnny how you can kiss', which they used to make fun of a shy carpenter who worked in the floor below. The team built up to 12 knitters, a linker, a presser, a finisher and a foreperson. It was very satisfying both for us and for the town's officials that we had quickly achieved 16 full-time jobs.

I had to learn many new things – how to open a bank account, write a cheque, keep books, prepare wages, deal with Purchase Tax, find suppliers and, most importantly, to obtain customers.

Each day I took the three children to school before work and after school they came to the factory to do their homework. They soon became great friends of Mr Graham's children whose house was in the same yard as his workshop and our factory.

On a flying visit from New York to Vienna in the middle of 1950, Bernhard stopped over in London. He invited us to meet him for a dinner in his hotel, the Savoy. Although I had written to him a number of times since my return to Vienna in early 1947, I had not seen him for 14 years. I was excited as I headed off with mother and the children to meet him. He was delighted with the children and we compared our experiences over the long years since we had last met. He was optimistic about the future and took it as a foregone conclusion that I would forge ahead and make a success of my business. He made it clear that he would continue to help in every way that he could. His great business achievements and the passing years had not diluted his kind nature.

Later in the year, our foreperson suggested we should organise a factory outing to Dublin. We hired a bus and set off on our two-hour journey, crossing the border into the Irish Republic between Newry and Dundalk. I was surprised at how dowdily the girls were dressed. I was even more surprised when they boarded the bus in the late evening for the return trip. Their main reason for the trip became evident – to avail themselves of the absence of rationing in the South. They had all bought new outfits and shoes, had extra nylons stuffed into their bras and had left the old clothes behind. Luckily, the customs staff had gone home before our very late crossing of the border. I realised how innocent I was.

By Christmas we had accumulated enough of our rationed tea to make up a parcel for every girl with tea and other scarce commodities. When rationing eventually stopped we changed to presents such as mittens, scarves or purses. The staff, in turn, gave presents to Kurt and me and always sweets for our children. In later years, when I went abroad on selling trips, I always bought a present for everyone, such as key rings, scarves or necklaces. I particularly remember maple leaf brooches from Canada.

We lived very frugally at that time and there is no doubt that our war experiences helped to strengthen our resolve and had taught us how to get along with very little. Lunch was taken in the factory on a packing case and usually consisted of Camp coffee, pilchards or corned beef and some biscuits. The children, who had meals at school, complained that their pocket money of sixpence fell far short of the half-crown (2s 6d) which other children got.

The business grew steadily from the start. Shortly after we arrived in Kilkeel a Mr Hutchinson from Londonderry visited because his wife, who owned the wool shop, told him that we made diamond-patterned Argyle socks. He was looking for a supplier of tartan hose-tops and had brought a sample. These hose tops were basically stockings without feet worn by pipe bands who also wear knee-length stockings, called full-clan hose, to match the design of their tartan kilts. We set about the challenge of producing these, which required twisting of two colours into a marled yarn. Kurt devised a suitable gadget and, shortly after, we sent off the sample. Mr Hutchinson ordered a hundred pairs of hose-tops. He had to finance our working capital to make them. Five years later, on a trip to Londonderry to fetch Kurt's mother to live with us, I discovered that our financier, Mr Hutchinson, was a bus conductor who made pipe band outfits as a sideline.

A few months later I gauged that our production capacity merited a selling trip to London. It also offered a chance to spend a few days with mother, who then lived with the two cousins of father's and worked as a machinist in the rag trade. She had lots of friends who called and everyone offered some advice on how I should go about selling. As I did not know London at all, these suggestions were most welcome and became very useful.

My first call was at Gieves in Bond Street. Having sold to their Londonderry branch was a good reference. The buyer was impressed and so I got my first London order! Next I went to Austin Reed in Regent Street. 'Sorry madam. You will have to go to our buying office in Red Lion Square.' I walked up Regent Street and then along Oxford Street until I found the office. The buyer was friendly and, when I told him the size of our production capacity, he replied that he could take the whole output. However, he advised me never to put all my eggs in one basket and gave me a reasonable order. I returned to Kilkeel very happy that I had secured several months work.

As production increased with the skill of the staff, I went a number of times to London and got new and valuable customers amongst whom were Saxone Shoes, Dolcis Shoes and Horne Brothers and the Scotch House in Knightsbridge. On all visits I kept looking for potential customers. One day a display of tartans attracted my attention because we had just introduced socks in tartan colours. I walked into the shop and met the owner – a tall elegant man with white hair and striking blue eyes. He gave me a substantial order. A few years later, on a visit, I offered him stock. He was surprised that I had spare stock and, when I explained that it was taken back from a customer who hadn't paid me, he exclaimed, 'I'll bet it was a Jew. My partner and I don't like the Jews.' Without saying a word, I grabbed my samples and, as I was repacking them, he said, 'You don't mean to say you are Jewish.' He apologised profusely and, after stammering and stuttering through embarrassment, gave me a large order! From then on I got a substantial order twice a year for 30 years.

Then Mr Hutchinson from Londonderry recommended us to a bagpipe-maker in Belfast who needed hose for bands. He told me that I should advertise in trade journals and competition programmes. This proved a splendid idea which produced enquiries from all over Scotland. I decided to visit these people and went on a trip which covered Glasgow, Edinburgh, Stirling, Perth, Dundee, Aberdeen and Inverness. It was a wonderful way of seeing beautiful scenery and proved a very instructive and successful trip, which I repeated each spring for many years.

Our most important new client was the supplier of tartan outfits to the Royal family. They sent a man to Kilkeel to help us to achieve their standards in kilt hose. Kurt liked this area of our production and became a real expert. Later, when we lost out in the sock market because our hand-framed Argyle products couldn't compete with those made on Japanese automatic machines, Kurt decided to use our machines for kilt hose only. Soon we supplied them all over the world and still do, 40 years on. Wherever there are pipe bands or dancing schools, you will find Kilkeel hose. We supply customers in Scotland, England, Canada, the United States, Singapore, Australia and New Zealand.

I may have given the impression that all went very smoothly – always up and up. Of course, the reality was that we had many setbacks and worries. Nine months after starting in

Kilkeel – The Early Years: 1950–55

Kilkeel, Bernhard requested that I produce a statement of profits and a balance sheet. Luckily my teenage training in commercial school enabled me to work out the figures which showed a modest profit. However, cash flow was a constant worry and I could not understand why customers weren't paying promptly. I didn't know that you had to send out statements in order to get people to pay!

Next I found that we needed a toe-closing machine. When the machine arrived I tried to use it without ever having seen one before. I pushed the two open ends on to the circle of points and turned the handle. To my horror the sock came out all cut up by the cutting tackle. I wrote to the makers, 'Please send me a manual of instructions.' Their answer was, 'Our machines are foolproof!' Then I realised that one had to slip every single stitch carefully on a single point in an absolutely straight row. Only that way the cutter trimmed the waste rows above the chain stitch that joined the two sides of the toe. Of course, I could not train a girl until I had mastered the art myself, but eventually we got there. In fact my first linker did the job for us for nearly 40 years until her poor hands were too crippled by arthritis.

In 1951 Lotte's marriage was under stress and her husband Ernst was spending most of his time in Germany. She and her son Josef moved into a beautiful apartment in the Paddington area of London and sublet a number of rooms to make ends meet. That same year, mother, who had first applied for a visa in 1939, obtained her affidavit for entry into the United States and she fulfilled her dream of moving to California. Although 57 then, she was very determined and started a course in home nursing and learnt to drive. In due course she became an American citizen and worked full time as a home nurse until pension age. After that she became a wealthy lady's companion. The climate was much better for her than that in England and she seemed to enjoy life to the full in California amongst many friends and in the wider Jewish community. She decided to return to London in 1969, aged 75 but, sadly, died two months later.

In 1952 yarn prices doubled because of the Korean War. I could not obtain a viable price for the Argyle socks. I was deeply worried about what I would do with the staff and how I would keep going. I then noticed a lot of newspaper advertisements for berets, hoods and other headgear – English women had gradually discarded their wartime habit of wearing headscarves. I experimented with pull-on hats with pom-poms or fringes and made samples. I arranged to meet Bernhard Altmann in London during one of his visits to discuss my dilemma and the fact that the new products entailed a lot of hand-working. His view was that I should proceed if I could get the right price and he recommended a wholesaler who gave me a trial order. Later the wholesaler had a range designed by a French designer, which the wholesaler sold under his own label. I had to employ a lot more girls to do the hand work and, within a week, had doubled the workforce. As soon as more new samples were ready I went to London and returned with more orders and more ideas.

Gradually the sock trade recovered and the kilt hose was in demand all the time. We got specially dyed yarn from a Yorkshire factory which was prepared to make the small quantities that suited our output. The yarn was dyed to match the various tartans. Once we got a batch of black yarn and found the dye came off on to the workers' hands. I complained, as I could not jeopardise my quality, and refused to pay. I was taken to court. On my next London visit I mentioned this to my good friend, the buyer for Horne Brothers. The suppliers withdrew the case before it came to court. It transpired that the buyer was also a director of the suppliers. He had made it clear to his co-directors that they should not risk the reputation of their own firm, being accused in my defence of supplying substandard merchandise.

In 1952 I got desperate with our cramped living conditions, sharing a small house with another family with three children. We were refused a council house, that had been promised, because we had not yet lived in Northern Ireland for seven years. Nobody wanted to put up children. So we applied to move to Canada. However, we were turned down, because we were not British subjects.

Our next move was to try to have a house built. We knew a friendly local builder who had a very nice site available. When I applied for a mortgage, I was rejected because my fledgling business had not got a secure enough income. Just then I heard, by chance, of a vacant apartment across the road from our workshop. (The locals always used the term 'flat', rather than 'apartment'.) When I was told I would have to share a bathroom with another tenant, I refused, and suggested having a bathroom installed in our prospective apartment. The landlord agreed. I went about buying furniture bargains at auctions and bought the children's beds through an army surplus catalogue. Happy and confident, we moved in during May 1953.

During that year Bernhard suggested that I go to Vienna and train at his factory, learning how to make high-class sweaters. He was then employing hundreds of people there producing luxury knitwear for the United States. I spent two weeks in the large Viennese factory bringing cashmere sweaters through all the production processes and then I spent some time producing intricate patterns on an intarsia machine.

The next key development of my business was the delivery of ten intarsia machines from Vienna. These were bought with Bernhard's help, on the basis of payment when able to pay. I had to train new girls in the process and find a supplier of cashmere yarn. Gradually we produced cashmere intarsia sweaters which were the most intricate and expensive merchandise in the trade. As there was so much money involved in the garments, I didn't trust anyone and washed every garment myself, by hand, until eventually I found an appropriate washing machine. I soon gave up cashmere because it was too expensive for us and we used the machines for lambswool and for kilt hose.

We also produced intarsia garments in wool to match our socks. One London buyer suggested I should visit the London buying houses of overseas stores. With my selection of sock and sweater samples I first called at the office of Gimbels of New York, which also looked after Saks of Fifth Avenue and Nieman Marcus of Dallas. I was so proud to clinch the most important order of all – for the Christmas catalogue of Nieman Marcus, then the world's most prestigious department store. We had reached the top of the customer list! These visits developed an important export business with the best stores in New York and in other North American cities, including those in Canada, where Eatons were a customer. I was so proud to see our products displayed in places like Fifth Avenue.

The first year in our new apartment brought contentment, happiness and a new baby. Esther was born in 1954 to the delight of Kurt and myself and particularly the other children. Well before the baby was due I searched for a reliable person to look after it when I went back to work. By a sheer stroke of luck a wonderful lady, Mrs Cousins, was recommended to me. She was willing to take on the job. Her husband was a fisherman and her own daughter was nine, the same age as our Leah. Mrs Cousins started work promptly as soon as Esther and I came home from hospital and she stayed with us until long after Esther married in 1985. Eventually she had to

Kilkeel – The Early Years: 1950–55

retire for health reasons, but we remain close friends. They say that behind every successful man there is a woman. I can honestly say that without Mrs Cousins I could not have devoted as much time as I did to building up the business.

During these years, in spite of long working hours, I found time to join the bridge club, the tennis club and the Women's Institute. Often, too, I went swimming in the sea and many times was the only bather. The Women's Institute at that time had a good drama group and I was overjoyed when invited to take part in a play.

At the end of 1954, the landlord wanted to double the rent for our workshop in the loft. I then looked for larger premises, which I got at a reasonable rent of £120. This was a good move because it provided enough space to use properly all the intarsia machines and the workforce of over 30. Through the grapevine we obtained a doubling machine which mechanised the hand-twisting of marls for the kilt hose. It was a monster but we had the space. Built in 1892, it was fully functional, reasonably priced and it still does the job after more than a hundred years.

In 1955 the children were seventeen, fifteen, ten and one. As I had always dwelt on the delights of all those happy holidays of childhood and youth with our parents, I planned that I would give our own children a similar experience. I knew we were in the last year before the older ones would start to go their own way, so I booked a holiday for Ruth, Walter, Leah and myself. Baby Esther could be left at home in safety with Kurt and Mrs Cousins.

I booked us into a *Gasthof* a few bus stops from my beloved Salzburg. We went there during August – the time of the Music Festival – the *Festspiele*. We went to a number of performances although I think the children enjoyed our excursions even more. We visited the ice caves, a salt-mine, the Hellbrunn Palace and the Königsee. On the return journey we stayed for a few days in Paris in a little hotel behind the Etoile. Walter took a lot of memorable photographs and Ruth produced a splendid scrapbook. I had thoroughly enjoyed my first real holiday with the children.

21 · A Phase of Development: 1956–70

We had a splendid stand of intarsia sweaters, sock-sets and kilt stockings at the first and only knitwear exhibition in the Seymour Hall in London. It took place in late 1955 and was a prestigious trade event, opened by the television celebrity, Lady Isobel Barnet. During a lunch-break whilst Lotte looked after the stand, a Mr Strauss called and told her that he might be interested in acting as our export agent. I went to see him later in his office in the city and discovered he had worked for Harrods in South America and had excellent connections in both London and Paris. We discussed a sample range that he could offer foreign buyers and he insisted that he could increase our turnover figure. Over the years it rose more than 20-fold through both our efforts.

It took me until 1959 to repay Bernhard, and thereafter I bought additional machines at auctions. Over the years I reduced my debts to him as soon as I had spare funds. This was possible only because we lived very frugally throughout and I adopted the discipline of never having a bank overdraft. As we took a minimum out for living, I ploughed as much as possible back into the business.

In 1959 Aunt Joan sent me a full-page advertisement from the *New York Times* showing a collection of handknitted Aran sweaters. At that time they were a novelty there and only available from the B. Altman & Co. department store.

I loved the challenge of making similar Aran garments, but doubted if I would find enough handknitters who could produce the intricate patterns. Thus, I started with simpler styles which Aunt Joan sold for us in New York. I then moved on to make fully styled Aran sweaters and was surprised to find that local knitters were very good at producing them. Our handknitting output was to build up to a requirement of about 250 knitters, all working at home.

Our business in the United States was growing each year, and by the end of 1961 the time had come for me to make my first sales trip. I decided to bring something really novel and knitted a coat which matched a dress made by a local lady who produced high-fashion garments in handwoven tweeds. I had used the same yarn.

Walter drove me to Dublin airport on the first part of my journey. When we came to the Irish border the customs official insisted that I pay duty on my samples. He requested I list all and submit the list to the Dundalk customs post. Of course, I had some dollars, mainly traveller's cheques, and no pounds. We went to the Dundalk branch of my own bank and luckily the manager was a cricketing pal of his opposite number in Kilkeel. This procured the necessary funds to clear the documents back at the customs office. The delay and the icy roads created a nerve-racking experience as I thought I would miss my plane. I just made it, and as I settled into the flight thought the episode a most inauspicious start to my first American trip.

Arrival in New York provided a wonderful surprise. Mother had travelled from Los Angeles and she and Aunt Joan were there to meet me. Mother and I stayed in a hotel near Aunt Joan's office on Madison Avenue. Her office became my base for working and making appointments with buyers. The evenings were reserved for family and friends and two highlights were a visit to the (old) Metropolitan

A Phase of Development: 1956–70

Opera House to hear Tebaldi as Turandot, and a concert in Carnegie Hall.

It was a most rewarding trip. I made many contacts and I received orders from Brooks Brothers and Paul Stuart on Madison Avenue for socks, and an order for the dress and coat set from Lord and Taylors. When I returned, my weaver friend said, 'Are you crazy? We can never do all this work!' In the end we completed the order together.

I flew from New York to Toronto to visit Canadian stores. I visited the buyers of Robert Simpson and T. Eaton and was proud and thrilled to see my products displayed in these enormous elegant stores.

By 1964 my New York customers were looking for Shetland cardigans and sweaters. At that time we did not make them but I had heard of a knitter on the island of Yell in the Shetlands who could fill the gap. He produced beautiful garments in the traditional way on handflat machines and, because there was no electricity on the island, brushed them with a foot-operated device. On receipt of his garments, we added labels and buttons and despatched the finished product to New York. After a while the 'poor boy's look' – undersized and worn-out – was all the rage with young people in Britain and in France and so I decided we would move into our own Shetland sweater production. On my next trip to London I bought a few second-hand domestic knitting machines and started a new line of products.

By this time Ruth was an occupational therapist in London. Walter studied at Cranfield College in England. Ruth decided to try her luck in Israel, where she found work in a children's hospital. One day in 1964 we received a telegram from her: 'Got engaged. Prepare for wedding'. We arranged the wedding in London. By sheer good luck my mother came from the States to celebrate her 70th birthday with us at the same time, so she was present at the wedding of her oldest grandchild. Leah, who had only been two when we came to Northern Ireland, graduated in 1966 at Queen's University, Belfast, in Social Sciences. In 1971 she also went to Israel, got married and has lived there ever since.

A year later, in 1965, Ruth had a daughter, Alona. I went to see my first grandchild and made my first visit to Israel. The journey had great significance, not least for the fact that, as mother thought we had perished, she had the trees planted there, in our memory. My son-in-law showed me around Jerusalem but I was apprehensive as I approached the border with Jordan on top of Mount Zion. There was a lot of barbed wire and danger warnings. Although I hadn't heard of any incidents I was glad to get away. I also went on a bus tour for two days, when I visited a kibbutz and learnt about life there. The tour took in Sfad and went north to the Lebanese border where we saw the fields scorched by Syrian attacks from the Golan Heights. From there we went along the coast to Acco and Haifa, which was a very busy port. The tour was impressive and instructive – it emphasised to me the beauty of the country and how much had been achieved since 1948. I have managed to visit Israel every year since.

Since 1966 we had been looking for larger premises for our ever-expanding business. Through various lucky events we bought a derelict schoolhouse in 1967, which showed promise. Kurt drew up plans and we proceeded to renovate the schoolhouse, for which we qualified for a grant. We moved into the new factory during the annual July holidays in 1968. We now had our own place, all paid for. Our pride and joy was the new maple parquet floor and we had the luxury, at last, of central heating. Now we had the space to spread out.

In spring 1968, Brian Faulkner, the Northern Ireland Minister of Commerce, visited our stand at a trade show in Sweden and we told him of our new factory. Later, at a British

A Phase of Development: 1956–70

embassy reception there, I asked him if he would officially open our factory. He suggested that I write to his secretary and, a few weeks later, was told that he could come in October. We laid on a full-scale reception using caterers from Belfast and invited local dignitaries, friends, our London agent and a number of important customers. The minister in his speech said that I was a better salesperson than himself because I had succeeded in obtaining orders from Brooks Brothers in New York where he had failed. It was a most enjoyable start to a new era for us.

At the same time as we were requested to expand our product range, home-knitting machines were becoming popular with some local women. This combination provided a great opportunity to introduce new styles and designs and to increase production. Many women phoned seeking outwork, which, gladly, I never refused. It was mutually beneficial.

From then on I had to make regular trips by air to Britain and to the United States and Canada. I had gone to Glasgow and Edinburgh every spring since 1951 and at one point over three-quarters of the shops in Prince's Street, Edinburgh were customers. At Christmas I would send each buyer a pair of tartan socks in their own clan colour – like Davidson, Johnson, MacPherson.

Over the years the production of Aran sweaters grew. We had agents all over Northern Ireland serving teams of handknitters. We now could bring together these garments with a substantial range of intarsia sweaters in many styles in Shetland wool and lambswool.

Around that time I joined the Belfast Chamber of Commerce and decided to take part in every trade mission that was organised. There were considerable savings by going in an organised group. The first mission I joined was to Hong Kong and Japan. This was very instructive and interesting. I obtained orders in Hong Kong but in Japan I had my greatest success by securing a substantial contract for handknitted Aran sweaters from the largest department store in Osaka, the 'Hankyu'. They remain faithful customers to this day.

I decided to fly home via Russia for two reasons. I wanted to see from the air the land where I had spent five and a half years interned in camps and I wanted to see Moscow airport, where we were to have a stopover. I spent most of the flight kneeling on my window seat and looking down. All I could see was a vast snow-covered featureless waste with no trees and no people evident. I was disappointed but not surprised.

Through 1971 and 1972 we found it became almost impossible to compete with foreign machine-knitted Argyle socks. On the other hand, tartan stockings were in strong demand. Kurt proposed that we drop the sock production after 20 years and use all the sock-making machines for the production of custom-made tartan stockings. From then on we separated our duties; Kurt concentrated on the stockings and I focused on the ever-increasing range of sweaters. This division of labour worked perfectly for many years.

22 · A Phase of Growth: 1971–74

Kurt and I were both kept constantly busy with our new, and divided, duties. As tartan hose sales grew so did those of sweaters. The handknitted lines were constantly increasing, lambswool intarsia sweaters were in steady demand, but Shetland sweaters which were produced mainly on domestic machines by outworkers, took off in a phenomenal way. Each spring I enjoyed the creative challenge of producing a new range of designs. Using my knowledge of machine and staff capabilities I merged my ideas with those of customers and with the new colour ranges from yarn suppliers.

This growing level of business also required regular visits to key markets, where I would pick up ideas and get design advice from top stores. On my annual visit to the United States, new and existing customers offered ideas and advice on new styles and designs. As my customers included such names as Barneys, Bloomingdales, Saks, Brooks, Paul Stuart, Lord and Taylor and Kevin McLaughlin I got a wide and varied response.

Another new opportunity arose in 1973, with a trade mission to Australia. We had a few small customers there whom I wanted to visit and, of course, several friends and relations. We flew into Melbourne where I visited several of our existing customers. My special success was to establish new and lasting relations with the finest men's outfitter in this city.

Next we flew to Sydney. There I met for the first time a customer, in person, whom we had supplied for many years. I was royally received and treated to a drive around the lovely countryside and a fine lunch. I also met several of my relations whom I had not seen since 1938. This was moving and most enjoyable.

My most memorable meeting in Sydney was with Luz Mandl, Kurt's school friend in Vienna. It was Luz who introduced us to each other in 1932. I was delighted to see he had succeeded so well in Australia and had an attractive wife, a Viennese called Hansi, and a son and daughter. He had emigrated in 1936, worked at first in Wolongong but eventually started his own manufacturing business producing electrical parts. After he settled in Australia, he helped his sister's family flee from the Nazis.

Our mission returned via Hong Kong where I spent a whole day negotiating orders for a famous department store called Wong On for delivery in August. When I returned eventually to my desk in Kilkeel I found out that our London agent had placed orders which filled our total capacity. I had to inform Hong Kong that I would have to delay their delivery by two months – they could not accept that and cancelled.

23 · *A House of our Own*

By 1974 our finances indicated that we could think seriously about getting a house of our own. Each time I returned from a trip abroad it hit me how small and cold the rooms of our rented house were.

Kurt and I never thought of buying an existing house; we always dreamed of building the one we wanted. All the landowners I approached refused to sell us a site. One fine sunny day I wandered down through the wilderness behind the factory – the former school playingfield – and it struck me that we had the space and the beautiful view.

We agreed that this was an appropriate site. Kurt started drawing up plans and then we sought out a local builder. He gave us an estimate for Kurt's unconventional ideas. The main feature was to be a large living-room with a very wide window giving a panoramic view of the mountains and with an open staircase leading to an upper gallery leading to the bedrooms. A lot of timber was to be used, including parquet flooring. It took exactly one year from start to completion. On the first evening in our own new home I sat down in the living-room and when I looked around I could hardly believe that all this was really ours. We had waited for this moment for a very long time – from the day we were married, 39 years ago. By then we had been living and working in Kilkeel for 25 of those years.

Now we had the room to invite children and grandchildren to stay with us on holiday. Esther had finished her studies in Leicester and had started work in our factory. She was a key member of management as we now had 30 staff and hundreds of outworkers.

At Christmas 1975 we had our first large family gathering in the new house. Walter, with his wife Moira and their sons David and Richard came from Scotland where they had settled. Leah arrived with daughter Tali from Israel. She wanted her second child to be born in Kilkeel. Her son Moti arrived promptly in January 1976.

Over the next few years we had visits from Lotte and from friends and relatives from Sweden, Austria, the United States and Australia. During those years I developed a garden and put up a greenhouse so that we would have fresh vegetables and soft fruit. My 'Granny Jam' is very popular with all the children.

24 · *Winding Down: 1976–91*

In 1976 I noticed in an export magazine an advertisement by a Japanese importer, Washo Inc., looking for Shetland Argyle sweaters. As this was our forte, I immediately responded and secured an initial order. I welcomed the chance to broaden our market base and become less dependent on American customers, who took about three-quarters of our sweater sales. The new association proved very fruitful and the buyer, Sam Sugure, came each year to Kilkeel to agree the following season's supplies.

Esther had become a very valuable member of management and made it easier for me to go off on frequent selling trips. She had spent two years at Leicester Technical College and one year in a Scottish knitwear factory. She became a very effective and versatile supervisor at a time when our name was so well known in the trade that agents and designers approached us to do business.

In 1981 I read about a government scheme to alleviate unemployment amongst redundant managers. By now I was 65 and considered it a good idea to share some of my responsibilities and workload. I obtained the services of an ex-manager of a large mill, which had closed, and the government paid 90 per cent of his salary for the first year.

I had high hopes, which proved unfounded. He talked me into some rash expenditures and into recruiting a lot more staff. This recruitment was based on the wrong reason – the availability of training grants. We ended up with over 50 people – more than we required for our volumes. He did, however, introduce us to LEDU, a government agency which helps small firms to develop. We embarked on a five-year expansion plan which included extending facilities, new machines and more staff. We renewed the manager's contract for another year, as everything looked promising. However, he proved so unpopular with staff that our team-working was beginning to fall apart. I couldn't wait for the year to end and see the end of him. At that stage, Walter came over from Scotland on a part-time commuting basis and, when he wound up his affairs there, he joined the firm in a full-time management role.

Although I phased out my involvement, I must admit that I found it extremely difficult to let go of the reins of day-to-day management of something I had built up successfully from scratch. However, I knew this was essential.

With Walter now more involved, Esther suggested in 1983 that we take a trip to Vienna to see where her parents had come from and where they had spent their early years.

Although I took less direct interest in the business in the following years, I still made a point of going on important sales trips. In the spring of 1988 I went on my last extensive trip to Canada and the United States. By this time the recession had really started to bite and I hoped, by personal contact, to save some of our lost business. I visited six cities and ended up with only a few requests for samples which did not lead to any orders. Everyone was overstocked and not replenishing. At that time, also, buyers had ceased coming from America to London, partly because of their stock situation, and the very adverse exchange rate conditions.

During the 1980s, Esther made a tremendous contribution to the business. In 1985 she got married in Belfast and, for the

Winding Down: 1976–91

first time since our other three children had gone to live abroad , we had a complete family gathering. Ruth, Leah and families came from Israel and Walter and family from Scotland. Lots of friends and relations from England and the United States came for the joyous reception in Conway Hotel. After her marriage, Esther commuted from her home in Belfast to Kilkeel until her son arrived in 1989.

In 1991, aged 75, I retired from active work in the business. Walter was now in sole charge, although Kurt and I were nominal directors. Kurt, however, kept up an active involvement in the tartan hose. Since then I have been very occupied with house and garden, with grandchildren, travelling and writing.

25 · Postscript

In recent years there were a number of events which were significant landmarks in my life. My story would be incomplete without their mention.

The first major event was our golden wedding in 1986. The staff were keen to give us something we would really cherish for the rest of our lives. We decided that what we most wanted was a photograph of all the staff, not only to remember them by, but also to reflect the success we all had achieved. It turned out to be a beautiful photograph which I treasure with the mountains of Mourne in the background and the 50 or so staff and members of the family in the foreground. We had a party for the staff and one for our friends, particularly those from the local bridge club. The culmination of our celebrations took place in Jerusalem with all the children, grandchildren, Lotte and cousin Heidi and husband from New York. We still have a video of our festive dinner in Beth Ticho, a beautiful restaurant in an historic setting. All the grandchildren gave a song and dance performance.

The next big celebration was Kurt's 80th birthday in 1987. He was lulled into thinking that a few friends were coming along to play bridge. It turned out to be a surprise party with a lovely buffet. If he had known, he would never have agreed – in the end he was very pleased.

Postscript

Then, in 1996, we had two further celebrations with our family and a wide circle of friends: my eightieth birthday in June and our diamond wedding in November. In the dark days of our captivity, we could never have imagined reaching these wonderful milestones and seeing out the century.

Two years after I retired from the business, one of the saddest moments of my life came when dear Lotte died. Since mother's death in 1969, Lotte had become so special to me as the only other survivor of our family. She had been an inspiration to me in my youth and I always admired her free-spirited personality. She had an unfortunate marriage to a cruel husband which ended in separation and then was devastated when Josef, her only son, died of leukaemia in his early forties. Through her years in London she had a series of long-term employments, the last of which was with British Home Stores until pension age. In 1976 she met a very cultured Hungarian and thereafter they lived happily together. Sadly she suffered a stroke in 1988 from which she did not recover, and eventually the doctors diagnosed motor neurone disease. She suffered gradual immobility from then and was nursed with great love and affection by her Hungarian partner. She was released from her suffering when she died in February 1993. She had retained her optimism and sense of humour almost to the end.

Lotte's passing was my second parting from her. It brought back that awful moment as her train headed out of that platform in Vienna in the summer of 1938. It had been a momentous half century for all of us.

Kurt and I have been fortunate to have retained our good health and lucky to enjoy the challenges in our work. For many years I worked a 60-hour week, which was necessary to cover the jobs I could do only after factory hours. Often I took a break – bridge, swimming, gardening – which refreshed me enough to tackle effectively the administrative and designing tasks. During factory hours I kept close to all aspects of the production process and was always available to staff for advice and problem-solving.

I loved work but never considered myself a 'workaholic'. I believe that this was due partly to my outlook and to the fact that I started at 16 to work in an orderly and strict environment – so hard work was second nature to me. As I grew older I realised an active life was very fulfilling and has probably kept both of us fit and sharp right up until now. Although the pace has slackened, I find life and travel as interesting and vital as ever.

Over the years I developed the following basic ideas:

1. Trust people and expect the best from them, within reason. I am, by nature, an optimist who believes that the majority of people are trustworthy and mean well. Of course, I have been disappointed at times, but I still retain that point of view.
2. Keep a tight rein on finances. Always keep within your budget.
3. Learn to use the equipment so that your help is meaningful to your staff.
4. Cater for different tastes and markets by giving them what they want – not what you think they ought to want.
5. Don't put all your eggs in one basket – spread your risks by having a number of markets. Keep an open mind – be very receptive to new ideas.

The Library of Holocaust Testimonies

Out of the Ghetto
Jack Klajman

Jack Klajman was an eight-year-old in Warsaw when Germany invaded Poland. He survived the bombing of his home, the daily risks and hardships of smuggling across the walls of the Warsaw Ghetto and the deaths of his parents and siblings. He was a participant in the Warsaw Ghetto uprising, fled the ghetto through the sewers and survived on the streets of Warsaw posing as a Catholic boy. Written from the perspective of the child, this autobiography chronicles Jack's tragic, but compelling story.

1999   208 pages illus   0 85303 389 7   paper

Have You Seen My Little Sister?
Janina Fischler-Martinho

A vividly-told account of the author's childhood experiences of the Krakow Ghetto, this work details the loss of all her immediate family, except her older brother, with whom she escaped from the Ghetto during its final liquidation, via the sewers. An important theme in this moving tale is that of memory and loss; whilst memory may be painful, it is the only memorial to many of those who have been consumed by the *Shoah*.

1998   296 pages
0 85303 334 X   paper

The Children Accuse
Maria Hochberg-MariaD ska and Noe Grüss

This most unusual book contains evidence collected by the author in 1945 in Poland from children and teenagers who surfaced from hiding in forests and bunkers, and told the story of their survival as it happened. The interviews, expertly translated from the original Polish, document life in the ghettos, in camps, in hiding, in the resistance and in prison.

1996   316 pages   0 85303 312 9   flapped paper

My Heart in a Suitcase
Anne L. Fox

Immediately after Kristallnacht in 1938, the author, then aged twelve, was sent to safety in England. This book tells of her experiences in adjusting to an unfamiliar environment, living with Jewish and Gentile families on a primitive farm and at a progressive boarding school.

1996 reprinted 1997   170 pages   illus   0 85303 311 0   flapped paper

A Cat Called Adolf
Trude Levi
This is one Holocaust memoir which does not stop at survival but goes on to describe the lasting effects upon those survivors of their persecution, betrayal and suffering.

The author's wish in telling her story is that the lessons of the Holocaust are never forgotten and that the events she has recorded are never allowed to happen again.

> 'The reader cannot help but marvel at her resilience and adaptability.'
> *Jewish Chronicle*

1995 reprinted 1995, 1996 176 pages illus0 85303 289 0 flapped paper

A Child Alone
Martha Blend
This book describes the author's background in pre-*Anschluss* Vienna, through its annexation by Hitler, her passage to England as a *Kindertransport* nine-year-old and her gradual assimilation into England and English culture during and after the war years.

> 'compelling detail, giving an insight into how the Kindertransport children transcended the horrors of separation, guilt and uncertainty to lead full, if not altogether happy lives.'
> Riva Klein, *The Times Educational Supplement*

1995 168 pages illus 0 85303 297 1 flapped paper

An End to Childhood
Miriam Akavia
Written as fiction but based on fact, this book describes the efforts of a young Polish brother and sister to survive in secrecy and constant anxiety in Lvov, at a time when Jews were being rounded up and sent to the Ghetto – or worse.

> 'This deeply moving book vividly recreates the complex perils of occupied Poland. Fear is tangible.'
> *Jewish Chronicle*

1995 124 pages illus 0 85303 294 7 flapped paper

I Light a Candle
Gena Turgel with Veronica Groocock
Out of the ashes of the Nazi concentration camps came an extraordinary love story which caught the public's imagination at the end of World War II. This autobiography tells how the author survived the camps and met her husband, a sergeant working for British intelligence when he arrived to round up the SS guards for interrogation.
1995 160 pages illus 0 85303 315 3 flapped paper

From Dachau to Dunkirk
Fred Pelican
Born in Upper Silesia, the author was imprisoned before the war for the 'crime' of being a Jew. He subsequently served in the British Army, was nearly captured in Dunkirk and ended the war as an interpreter at BAOR (British Army on the Rhine) Headquarters, helping to investigate war crimes.
1993 224 pages illus 0 85303 253 X

My Lost World
A Survivor's Tale
Sara Rosen
An account of how a young girl from Krakow was able to survive the Tarnow ghetto and escape to Bucharest, this book tells the story of what was once the largest Jewish community in the world.

> 'The Holocaust wiped out not just a way of life, a tradition, and Rosen's story is in remembrance of this. She escaped through a series of risky adventures and was among one of the first survivors to enter Palenstine.'
> *Jewish Chronicle*

1993 reprinted 1996 320 pages 0 85303 254 8 flapped paper

My Private War
One Man's Struggle to Survive the Soviets and the Nazis
Jacob Gerstenfeld-Maltiel
The author experienced the first 21 months of Soviet rule in the Polish town of Lvov and then, from June 1941, the nightmare of Nazi genocidal policies. He survived in a most unusual way, by disguising himself as a civilian auxiliary of the German Army.

> 'His closeness to the events he describes enables him to provide a wealth of detail. He recreates the unbearable tension of life.'
> *Jewish Chronicle*

1993 336 pages 0 85303 260 2 flapped paper

Books of Related Interest

Holocaust Literature
Schulz, Levi, Spiegelman and the Memory of the Offence

Gillian Banner

Foreword by Colin Richmond

Holocaust Literature provides an evaluation of the dynamics of memory in relation to representations the Holocaust. It examines the compulsion to remember, the dilemmas of representation, and the relationship between memory, knowledge and belief in the works of Bruno Schulz, Primo Levi and Art Spiegelman.

Holocaust Literature combines close readings of individual works, supported by a sound theoretical framework, with a consideration of the varieties of memory, and the particular problems of Holocaust memory. This approach reveals a 'hierarchy of remembrance' which exemplifies the changing nature of representations of Holocaust memory.

2000 184 pages 14 b/w illus

0 85303 364 1 cloth

0 85303 371 4 paper

Parkes-Wiener Series on Jewish Studies

Double Jeopardy
Gender and the Holocaust

Judith Tydor Baumel

In this collection of essays the author examines the Holocaust from the perspective of gender and focuses on the discourse between gender and identity. Social interaction in crisis, mutual assistance groups, leadership and martyrdom are all topics that are explored.

An extensive multi-lingual bibliography of sources and studies dealing with various gender-related aspects of the Holocaust makes this book a necessary reference tool.

1998 320 pages
0 85303 346 3 cloth
0 85303 345 5 paper
Parkes-Wiener Series on Jewish Studies